THE SUBJECT OF
SCHIZOPHRENIA
- ALL YOU WANT TO KNOW
ABOUT THE ILLNESS

THE SUBJECT OF
SCHIZOPHRENIA

- ALL YOU WANT TO KNOW
ABOUT THE ILLNESS

B. S. RUOSS

To order additional copies of this book, contact:
Xlibris
1-888-795-4274
www.Xlibris.com
Orders@Xlibris.com
810880

CONTENTS

Dedicated *To*

Michael, who has always been loving and
supportive when I encountered my struggles
with schizophrenia and depression.

FOREWORD

The idea, or rather the need for writing a book on Schizophrenia didn't come to me by accident. I have considered writing it since my book "Betty's Battle – A True Story of Depression and Schizophrenia" was published.

You see, I am a person who suffers from schizophrenia and have suffered with it most of my adult life. After having been in many psychiatric hospitals, and prescribed many different types of psychotropic medications during this time, it wasn't until nine years ago when I was prescribed a combination of medications which helped me tremendously with my psychosis. Right now, I have no signs of depression or schizophrenia, and by the grace of God, I can now say that my condition is in remission and under control.

This book is meant to be for informational and educational purposes only. It is not meant to be a substitute for professional advice. It is a guide book for those who are interested in the subject of schizophrenia. All information in this book is based on what I have learned about the illness through studies, therapy and what I have experienced as a person with schizophrenia. Hopefully it will give you a broader view of what schizophrenia entails.

PART I

BACKGROUND OF SCHIZOPHRENIA

In decades past, it was often believed people who had psychological disorders, or those exhibiting strange behavior, (as with schizophrenia) were possessed by demons. Those people were forced to take part in exorcisms, were imprisoned, or executed, and were not welcome in society. Many of the mentally ill people were killed and often burned at the stake after being accused of being witches or under the influence of witchcraft.

Mental Asylums were built to house the mentally ill, but the patients received little to no treatment. Patients were often abused and neglected. Many of the methods used to treat them were cruel. For extreme cases of mental illness a procedure used to drill a small hole was made in the afflicted individual's skull to release spirits from the body. Most people died from this treatment.

Asylums were filthy and in deplorable conditions. People were locked in closets, chained to the walls, and were poorly fed and beaten.

In 1841, Dorothea Dix, who was a pivotal figure in mental health reform, argued for more humane treatment of the mentally ill. Dix visited every public and private institution which was accessible documenting the conditions she found. Her reports with her findings were presented to the legislature of Massachusetts demanding that officials take action toward reform. As a result of her efforts, funds were made available for a state mental hospital in Worcester. Dix spent the next 40 years lobbying U.S. and Canadian legislators to establish state hospitals for the mentally ill. In the mid-1960's, the deinstitutionalization movement gained support and asylums were closed. Instead of asylums, we now have psychiatric hospitals run by state governments and local community hospitals.

Instead of long-term stays in the hospital, the emphasis is on short-term stays. Many people suffering from mental illness are not hospitalized today. A person suffering with symptoms could speak with a primary care physician, who would more than likely refer him or her to someone who specializes in therapy. The person can receive outpatient mental health services from a variety of sources. These sources could be a psychologists, psychiatrists, marriage and family therapists, school counselors, clinical social workers, and religious personnel. These therapy sessions would be covered through insurance, government funds or paid for by the person.

Although the term "schizophrenia" was not used until the early 20th century, the disorder has existed for a great many years and has been found in all types of societies.

In Western society, "madness" or "insanity" was not generally regarded as a health problem until the early 19th century. The Dorothea Dix movement offered more humane treatment to the mentally ill and made it possible for them to receive more scientific, medical treatment. The mentally ill were unchained, released from prisons, and given more appropriate care.

Emil Kraepelin, (1856-1926), was a German psychiatrist who is recognized as the founder of modern psychiatry and psychopharmacology. He believed that the basic origin of psychiatric disease was linked to biological and genetic malfunction. Kraepelin also developed a classification system for mental illness, which helped to bring about future classifications.

Dr. Kraepelin used the term "dementia praecox" for the people who had symptoms that we now recognize as schizophrenic symptoms. In

1897 Kraepelin classified schizophrenia as a distinct mental disorder. He was the leader to make a distinction in the psychotic disorders called dementia praecox and manic depression. He believed that dementia praecox was primarily a disease of the brain, and a form of dementia (today referred to as schizophrenia).

Eugen Bleuler, (1857-1939}, was a Swiss psychiatrist who coined the term "schizophrenia" in 1911. He was the first person to describe the symptoms of schizophrenia as "positive or "negative." Bleuler changed the name "dementia praecox" to "schizophrenia" because the illness was not a dementia, and the name dementia praecox was misleading. The term schizophrenia has been commonly used since then.

PART II

DEFINITION OF SCHIZOPHRENIA

Schizophrenia is a serious mental disorder in which people observe reality abnormally. Psychiatrists, neurologists and other medical professionals have, through research and observation, determined that schizophrenia is a disease of the brain, a mental illness and a psychotic disorder. As of today, there is no physical or lab test to diagnose schizophrenia. A psychiatrist generally comes to the diagnosis based on clinical symptoms.

Schizophrenia can cause hallucinations, delusions, and disordered thinking and behavior that affect daily functioning, and can be disabling. People with schizophrenia may require lifelong treatment. Early treatment may help get symptoms under control before more serious complications or conditions develop and may help improve the long-term outlook.

Schizophrenia affects probably one-percent of the population in the United States at any given time. There are two-million people that are diagnosed with schizophrenia at any given year.

Schizophrenia is a complex illness. Many people have heard of it but not many, including medical professionals, fully understand the illness. The best way to understand what schizophrenia means is to study it by its individual pieces.

Schizophrenia is an individualized illness. It is different for every person who lives with it. No two people experience the same symptoms. It is actually a group of symptoms and features than a single illness. Each case of schizophrenia has a unique combination – in terms of severity, duration, prominence of positive, negative and other symptoms. It is a very serious mental illness that interferes with a person's perception, thoughts, feelings, cognitive processing and behavior.

One thing that is consistent for everyone suffering with schizophrenia is that schizophrenia interferes in life. It can affect functioning in one or more life areas listed below:

- Work
- School
- Relationships
- Social activities
- Self-care

When schizophrenia is present, the person's symptoms may include delusions, hallucinations, trouble with thinking and concentration, and lack of motivation.

Just as an individual, not suffering from schizophrenia, may view the world from their own perspectives, people who suffer with schizophrenia, also, have their own perceptions of reality. Their view of the world is very different from the reality seen and shared by those who are not affected by the illness.

Living in a world that appears distorted and having no reliable landmarks that we all use to anchor ourselves to reality, a person with schizophrenia may feel confused and anxious. This person may seem distant, detached, or preoccupied, or he or she may even sit for hours without moving and not making a sound. Or the person may move around constantly, wide awake, vigilant, and alert. A person with schizophrenia may display different kinds of behavior at different times.

There are positive and negative symptoms of schizophrenia, as well as cognitive symptoms. These symptoms usually begin between the ages of 16 and 30. Men can exhibit symptoms earlier than women.

SYMPTOMS

POSITIVE SYMPTOMS: Positive symptoms refer to a distortion of a person's normal thinking and functioning. They are "psychotic" behaviors. People with positive symptoms are sometimes unable to tell what's real from what is imagined. They may "lose touch" with reality. POSITIVE SYMPTOMS INCLUDE:

HALLUCINATIONS: The schizophrenic person's world may be filled with hallucinations. The person may sense things that do not really exist. The person may sense smells that are really not there. He or she may hear voices instructing them to do certain things. The person may see people or objects that are not really there; or feel invisible fingers touching his or her body.

Hearing voices that other people don't hear is the most common type of hallucination in schizophrenia. The voice(s) may carry on a conversation, describe the person's activities, warn of upcoming dangers, or tell the person what to do. Because the Schizophrenic person hears voices that no one else hears, it is usually a long time before family or friends notice a problem.

DELUSIONS: Delusions are basically false ideas that the schizophrenic person believes to be true, but which cannot be, and to which the person firmly adheres despite well-reasoned arguments. Sometimes delusions in schizophrenia are quite bizarre – for instance, the person may believe that he or she is a famous person such as the President, or that he or she may have super powers… like Jesus Christ. He or she may believe that people on television are directing special messages (comments or gestures) specifically at him or her, or are broadcasting the individual's thoughts aloud to other people. Delusions of persecution, which are common in paranoid schizophrenia, are false and irrational beliefs that a person is being cheated, harassed, poisoned, or conspired against. The person believes that they are in danger—that other people are trying to hurt them. The individual may believe that he or she, or a member of the family or other group, is the focus of this imagined persecution.

DISORGANIZED THINKING: Often times, the schizophrenic person's thinking may become "disorganized." The person may endure many hours of not being able to "think straight"...... jumping from one topic to another in a way that is totally confusing to others. The person may make up words or phrases that only have a meaning to him or her who created it. The person may talk in rhymes even if it doesn't mean anything. Thoughts may come and go rapidly. More than likely, the person may not be able to concentrate on one thought for a very long time and may be easily distracted, unable to focus attention.

The person may not be able to sort out what is relevant and what is not relevant to a situation. He or she may not be able to connect thoughts into logical sequences, as thoughts may be disorganized and fragmented. This lack of logical continuity of thought can make conversation very difficult and contribute to social isolation. If someone cannot make sense of what an individual is saying, they tend to become uncomfortable and are likely to leave that person alone.

MOVEMENT DISORDERS: Movement disorders may appear as agitated body movements. Sometimes the person with movement disorder may make the same motions over and over again. At other times, a person may stop moving or talking for a while, or act as others aren't even there. This is a rare condition call "catatonia."

NEGATIVE SYMPTOMS: Negative symptoms refer to "things you no longer do or have stopped doing." Negative symptoms also refer to difficulty showing emotions or inability to function normally. When a person with schizophrenia has negative symptoms, it may look like depression. People with negative symptoms may:

- Exhibit a Lack of Emotional Response –
  The person has a "flat affect" shows no signs of emotions, such as lack of facial expressions, or restricted or blank facial expressions; shows neither sadness nor happiness; and speaks in monotone.

- Withdrawal or Depression –
  The person isolates themselves socially; withdraw or lack the ability to experience pleasure.

- No Initiative or Drive –
  The person may lack self-care by neglecting personal hygiene and lacks the motivation.

- Lack of Interest –
  The person may have difficulty beginning activities; and is unable to follow through with any plans.

SUBTYPES

COGNITIVE SYMPTOMS: Cognitive symptoms are problems relating to memory and concentration. These symptoms are not easy to see, but they can make it hard for people to have a job or take care of themselves. Cognitive symptoms include:

- Inability to understand and use information to make decisions.
- Not being able to use information immediately after learning it.
- Unable to focus; trouble paying attention.

Schizophrenia was once divided into five subtypes. In 2013 these subtypes were eliminated. Today, schizophrenia is one diagnosis. The subtypes of schizophrenia, helped professionals recognize what someone is experiencing and helped in the creation of a treatment plan tailored to each individual. Further, knowing these traits was thought to help others understand what someone with schizophrenia was going through, thus increasing empathy and the ability to offer support. However, the subtypes are no longer used as clinical diagnosis. They were found not helpful to clinicians because patients' symptoms often changed from one subtype to another causing overlapping of subtype symptoms, which blurred distinctions among the five subtypes and decreased their validity. The subtypes used were:

- Catatonic Schizophrenia –
  This subtype is attributed with disturbances in movement as well as extreme behaviors. The individual may exhibit slow motion, rigidity, even immobility. The individual may ignore the presence of others, or may repeat actions of others, or repeat others words/ phrases.

- Paranoid Schizophrenia –
  Paranoid schizophrenia is identified as the most common subtype. Auditory hallucinations and/or delusions (false beliefs), anxiety, aloofness, and argumentative behavior are present in this subtype. None the less, this type has the best prognosis of all the subtypes.

- Disorganized Schizophrenia –
  This subtype most closely fit the stereotype of what we think a crazy person would look like. The greater attributes for this subtype are disorganized odd behavior and speech; with flat or inappropriate affect; and unkept appearance (often wears inappropriate clothing for the weather.) Disorganized Schizophrenia has the worst prognosis of all the subtypes.

- Residual Schizophrenia –
  When positive symptoms are suppressed to a small degree with very little of them showing; the individual may show some signs of the illness, but are not showing any positive symptoms; the positive symptoms like hallucinations are very minimal and for the most part are none existent. This can mean the illness is under control and the person is beyond better.

- Undifferentiated Schizophrenia –

When the individual has a mixed set of symptoms, which involves features from other types of schizophrenia present, but he doesn't display enough traits of each to be considered paranoid, catatonic or disorganized.

The complexity of schizophrenia may help explain why there are misconceptions about the disease. Contrary to what many people believe, schizophrenia is not a "split personality" or "multiple-personality." There is common belief that schizophrenia is the same as "split personality" – a Dr. Jekyll-Mr. Hyde character switch. This is not an accurate description of schizophrenia. As a matter of fact, split or multiple personality is an entirely different disorder that is quite rare.

Anyone can develop schizophrenia. It affects men and women equally in all ethnic groups. Young children can develop schizophrenia, but it is rare before adolescence. More research is needed to clarify the relationship of schizophrenia occurring in childhood to that occurring in adolescence. Although some people who later develop schizophrenia may have seemed different from other children at an early age, the psychotic symptoms of schizophrenia (for example, hallucinations, delusions and incoherence) are rarely seen in children.

The early signs of schizophrenia mostly happen in the teen years. The signs can be difficult to spot because these early schizophrenia signs are similar to behaviors often seen in teens in general. If the very earliest schizophrenia signs occur before the age of 16, they may not become noticeable until between the ages of 16 and 30. The signs of a teen developing schizophrenia may include:

- Start getting bad grades in school.
- Change friends.
- Have trouble sleeping.
- Be irritable or moody.
- Cognitive impairment (may appear in childhood)

As a person gets older, the symptoms of schizophrenia tend to become more pronounced because schizophrenia becomes a full-blown illness. At this point, signs of schizophrenia include:

- Social isolation and withdrawal.
- Irrational, bizarre or odd statements or beliefs.
- Increased paranoia or questioning others' motivations.
- Becoming more emotionless.
- Hostility or suspiciousness.
- Increasing reliance on drugs or alcohol (in an attempt to self-medicate).
- Lack of motivation.
- Speaking in a strange manner unlike themselves.
- Inappropriate laughter.
- Insomnia or oversleeping.
- Deterioration in their personal appearance and hygiene.
- Excessive, pointless muscle activity; repetition of movement or speech.
- Inappropriate or lack of mood.

These schizophrenia signs and symptoms often make working impossible resulting in periods of joblessness and even homelessness. However, there may be times when the person is not suffering from schizophrenia symptoms. The person is in remission then life can resume as normal.

Behaviors of schizophrenia can also severely impact home and social life. The tendency to withdraw from others and exhibit inappropriate mood behaviors can make relationships difficult. When the person is hearing voices or being delusional, the person with schizophrenia is likely not able to participate in home and family life and chores. In fact, a family often starts to revolve around the person with schizophrenia because schizophrenia symptoms take so much effort to manage from all involved.

It's important to remember though, that those negative outcomes tend to present themselves when the person is not being treated for their schizophrenia symptoms.

Loved ones and friends may spot early warning signs long before the primary symptoms of schizophrenia occur. During this initial pre-onset phase, a person may seem without goals in their life, becoming increasingly eccentric and unmotivated. They may also isolate themselves and remove themselves from family and friends situations. They may stop engaging in other activities that they used to enjoy, such as hobbies or volunteering.

While there is no guarantee that one or more of these symptoms will lead to schizophrenia, a number of them occurring together should be cause for concern, especially if it appears that the individual is getting worse over time. This is the ideal time to act to help the person.

Research has shown even though schizophrenia affects men and women about equally, it may have an earlier onset in males. Schizophrenia in men tends to develop between the ages of 15-20 whereas for women, schizophrenia tends to develop between 20-25 years of age. Moreover, not only does schizophrenia in men occur earlier, men are often hit harder by the disease.

Men diagnosed with schizophrenia are more likely to suffer more with the following symptoms:

- Lack of drive or purpose; a tremendous sense of inertia.
- Lack of desire to plan and complete tasks or projects.
- Making decisions.

Men with schizophrenia may also react less positively to medication.

Because the symptoms of schizophrenia are less severe in women, women are more likely to:

- Marry
- Hold down a job.

Men are more likely to have trouble with joblessness and homelessness.

PART III

CAUSES OF SCHIZOPHRENIA

Schizophrenia is no one's fault. No one is to blame and there's nothing you did to cause it. The causes of schizophrenia are complex and not completely understood at this time. It is likely the result of complex interplay of many different factors. While the exact cause is not known, experts think that a combination of family history (genetics), environmental factors, and certain chemical imbalances in the brain (that causes messages in the brain to get mixed up), history of abuse or neglect, may be risk factors for developing schizophrenia. Researchers have spent millions of hours (and many hundreds of millions of dollars) studying this condition. The more they learn, the more it becomes evident that the condition is far more complex than anyone realized.

Schizophrenia – like all mental illness – runs in families, but no single gene is thought to be responsible. Different combinations of genes make one more vulnerable to the condition. However, having these genes does not necessarily mean you will develop schizophrenia. Schizophrenia occurs in only one percent of the general population. A person who has a family history of schizophrenia has a greater risk of developing this condition. People who have a close relative with schizophrenia are more likely to develop the disorder than are people who have no relatives with the illness. A child whose parent has schizophrenia has about a 10 percent chance of developing schizophrenia themselves. Where there are identical twins, if one twin develops schizophrenia, the other twin has a one in two chance of also developing it. People who have a distant-relative or second-degree relative such as, aunts, uncles, grandparents, or cousins, with the disease also develop schizophrenia more often than the general population. Whenever people with schizophrenia have no family history of it, scientists believe that in these cases, a gene may have changed and made the condition more likely.

Research shows that a person with schizophrenia may have been affected by situations during the prenatal stages of their life. Certain conditions contribute to later development of schizophrenia. Prenatal difficulties that are thought to increase the risk of schizophrenia are:

- The lack of oxygen during the mother's pregnancy or at birth.
- The mother's exposure to viruses, bacteria or toxins during pregnancy.
- Being exposed to Lead during pregnancy.
- Experiencing a high level of stress, such as family stress, social or fetal development stress.
- Smoking during pregnancy.
- Malnutrition during pregnancy.
- Having an older father.
- Premature labor.
- A low birth weight (such as abnormal fetal development.)

This theory is not meant to blame a mother for an offspring who developed schizophrenia. It is still being studied to find the right answers.

Studies show that people with schizophrenia brains show subtle differences in how it is structured. These changes may not be seen in everyone with schizophrenia. Nonetheless, they suggest schizophrenia may also be a disorder of the brain. The brains of people with schizophrenia look different than those of healthy people. The fluid-filled cavities at the center of the brain, which are known as ventricles, are larger in some people with schizophrenia. Individuals with schizophrenia have a reduced volume of gray matter in the brain, mainly in the temporal and frontal lobes. Neuroscientists have discovered that there is a loss of up to 25% of gray matter in some areas. People with the most loss of brain tissue, had the worst schizophrenic symptoms, such as hearing voices, psychotic thoughts, depression and hallucinations. There is no reason to lose hope because of the significant loss of gray matter in the brain.

Neurotransmitters are chemicals that are responsible for communicating information in the brain. These neurotransmitters are thought to be a cause in the development of schizophrenia. People who have schizophrenia brains show imbalances with neurotransmitters (messengers) serotonin and dopamine. Research has shown schizophrenia may be caused by a change in the level of these two neurotransmitters.

Research has shown that, in people with schizophrenia:

- Ventricles, which are spaces in the brain, were larger.
- The medial temporal lobes, which are parts of the brain that deal with memory, were smaller.
- The connections between brain cells were fewer.
- Brain tissue in people with schizophrenia after death showed that their brain structure was different than how it looked at birth.

Drug abuse can impact a person's risk for developing mental illness. Many of the recreational drugs can increase the risk of developing schizophrenia. Certain drugs, such as cannabis, cocaine, LSD or amphetamines, may trigger symptoms of schizophrenia in people who are susceptible. If you are using cocaine or amphetamines this may very well lead to psychosis, and may also cause a relapse in people with schizophrenia who has recovered from an earlier episode.

Stressful events can trigger schizophrenia. Although, these triggers are not direct causes of schizophrenia, they can trigger its development in someone already vulnerable to it. These psychological triggers of schizophrenia results from stressful life events such as:

- Bereavement (losing a loved one or relative.)
- Losing your home.
- Loss of your job.
- The need to change jobs.
- Getting a divorce.
- Ending of a significant relationship.
- Abuse (sexual, physical or emotional.)

Research links sexual, physical and emotional abuse, school bullying and parental neglect to schizophrenia in adulthood. The risk of developing schizophrenia and other forms of psychosis increased in line with the amount of abuse or trauma a child went through. Children who encounter severe forms of abuse are more likely to develop schizophrenia and related psychoses in later life compared with children who do not experience abuse. This finding is based on a study that has brought together psychiatric data from almost 80,000 people. However, any type of abuse which occurred at any stage in life can trigger schizophrenia for individuals who are already susceptible to developing it.

Even though research continues to better understand the causes of schizophrenia, the good news is that this illness can still be treated successfully.

PART IV

SCHIZOPHRENIA AND VIOLENCE

News and entertainment media often relate mental illness to criminal violence. Contrary to what is said, people with schizophrenia are not usually violent or dangerous. They are more likely to be victims of violence. As a matter of fact, most violent crimes are not committed by people with schizophrenia. Don't assume that a person with a mental illness, as with schizophrenia, is a serial killer or a deranged killer you might see in a movie.

Studies indicate, if the person with mental illness had a criminal record, substance abuse or alcohol problem before being diagnosed with schizophrenia, he may possibly be prone to violence. Schizophrenics have no higher incidence of being violent than the rest of the population.

Hostility and aggression are sometimes associated with schizophrenia, although it is important to note that the vast majority of individuals with schizophrenia are not aggressive. More typically, they are withdrawn and prefer to be left alone. However, some symptoms are associated with violence, such as delusions of persecution. People with paranoid and psychotic symptoms, which can become worse if medications are discontinued, may also be at higher risk for violent behavior. Most violent crimes are not committed by persons with schizophrenia, and most persons with schizophrenia do no commit violent crimes. Substance abuse significantly raises the rate of violence in people with schizophrenia but also in people who do not have any mental illness. When and if a person with schizophrenia becomes violent, the violence is usually directed at family members and friends and tends to take place at home.

PART V

SCHIZOPHRENIA AND SUICIDE

Suicide is a problem for some people with schizophrenia. Studies show, a person with schizophrenia is more likely than other people to attempt suicide in the general population. On average, about one out of ten schizophrenic patients commit suicide. This is due in large part to depression and paranoia that characterize the disorder. Some people hear voices telling them to hurt themselves or some may experience periods of depression. Many of the warning signs of a schizophrenic person with depression who has suicidal thoughts include:

- Making final arrangements (they may give away possession, draw up a will or say goodbye to friends or loved ones).
- They may talk about death or suicide (saying, "I wish I was dead," or "Dead people are happier than us," or "It would be nice to go to sleep and never wake up again."
- Self-injury (cutting themselves on the wrist or throat, or burning themselves with a cigarette).
- Having a sudden lift of spirits or mood (this can happen when a person has decided to end their life and feels better because they have decided to do so).

People with schizophrenia are more likely to commit suicide if they are young, male, white, under age 30, and never married. The person is also more likely to commit suicide if they developed depression after the diagnosis of schizophrenia, and has a history of alcohol or substance abuse, or a history of past suicide attempts.

Suicide is also likely If the person has a higher IQ or has been a high achiever during teen years and as a young adult, or in the first 6 to 9 months after they started first taking medication when they are thinking more clearly and realize that they have schizophrenia and all the negative aspects that this connotes.

Even though men are more likely than women to commit suicide, women are more likely to attempt it but are unsuccessful. Men are more likely to commit suicide by fatal means such as using a gun or jumping off a tall building, whereas women are more likely to take an overdose of pills or cut themselves.

Suicide is also more likely in someone who is:

- Hopeless.
- Socially isolated.
- Living in a hospital or after being discharged.

Quite frequently the risk of suicide goes up when the schizophrenic patient leaves the hospital. This can happen when the person sees the staff people and other patients at the hospital as the central people in their life, and then feel hopeless without them when he or she leaves the hospital.

In addition to the above, other attributing factors to suicide among people with schizophrenia are:

- Being very upset and impulsive.
- Negative outlook on life.
- Sense of worthlessness.
- Family history of suicide.
- Past or present history of depression.

- Negative attitudes toward medication and not following their Treatment Plan.
- Not being able to work and being dependent on others.

Suicide prevention can be hard to do, because people with schizophrenia can sometimes act on suicidal thoughts suddenly and without warning. With this being, it is necessary that health care workers, caregivers, family members, and friends be aware and know what to do. Keep an eye out for signs that the person feels hopeless or that they have suffered a loss. If you know someone who talks about suicide, help him or her find help quickly. You can help by:

- Letting them know they are not alone and that you care about them.
- Offering your support by helping to solve the problem with other solutions rather than suicide.
- Showing a willingness to listen to them.
- Not talking on the value of life.
- Being available if they need you.
- Showing interest in what they are saying.
- Moving all means out of reach if you are near them, such as guns, knives, pills.
- Not acting shocked - Remaining calm.

If you feel you cannot help the crisis situation and require assistance, you may telephone, or have the suicidal person telephone the below listed hotlines for help. They are open 24/7.

- 1-800-273-8255 (1-800-273-TALK) – National Suicide Prevention Lifeline
- 1-800-784-2433 (1-800-SUICIDE) – National Hope Line Network
- 1-866-488-7386 (1-866-4U-TREVOR – (Aimed at gay and questioning youth).
- Call 911 (Go to the nearest hospital emergency).

PART VI

TREATMENTS FOR SCHIZOPHRENIA

MEDICATIONS

There is no cure for schizophrenia. However, antipsychotic medications have proven to be the most effective treatment for schizophrenia. Antipsychotic medications change the balance of chemicals in the brain and help control symptoms.

The first antipsychotic medications for mental illness were introduced in the early 1950's. They were chlorpromazine, haloperidol, and fluphenazine. Since that time, dozens of other medications have followed.

There are two groups of antipsychotic medications. The older group of medications are called "first generation," conventional'" or "typical" antipsychotics. These medicines include:

- Thorazine
- Prolixin
- Haldol
- Trilafon
- Mellail

- Navane
- Stelazine

The newer antipsychotics medications are called "second-generation, or "atypical. They are less likely to block dopamine and cause movement disorders. However, they can increase the risk of weight gain and diabetes. With medication intervention and making a change in nutrition and exercise can be a help in addressing these side effects. The atypical group of medicines include:

- Abilify
- Saphris
- Clozaril
- Fanapt
- Latuda
- Zyprexa
- Invega
- Seroquel
- Risperdal
- Geodon

Antipsychotic medicines are usually helpful however, they can cause side effects. Your doctor must decide whether to treat your condition with first or second generation antipsychotic medication. Doctors normally would choose second generation antipsychotics over first generation antipsychotics because of the side effects they carry. First generation, conventional, or typical antipsychotics can severely affect body movements. The first generation antipsychotics side effects can be;

- Feelings of restlessness or "jitters."
- Muscle cramps that are painful.
- Tremor.
- Slowed, involuntary and repetitive movements.
- Higher levels of hormone prolactin.

The atypical or second generation antipsychotic medicines are associated with weight gain and you may have trouble keeping your blood sugar and cholesterol levels under control.

The most common side effects of all antipsychotic drugs are:

- Blurred vision.
- Dry mouth.
- Drowsiness.
- Constipation.
- Sleepiness (sedation).
- Dizziness.

The most serious side effects from long-term use of both the first generation (older) and second generation (newer) medications are movement disorders called tardive dyskinesia (TD). This disorder makes your tongue, facial, and neck muscles move uncontrollably. This can be permanent. Notify your doctor or pharmacist of any new, persistent or worsening side affects you may have. Many side effects can be managed.

Side effects are often treated by lowering the dosage of the antipsychotic medication, by trying a different medication, or by treating the side effect directly with additional medication, such as a Cogentin. Your doctor may keep switching medications, or adjusting dosages. This is not meant to be experimenting on you. By trial-and-error he would eventually find a combination that works. Remember only your doctor should determine whether to raise, lower or change your dosage.

People with schizophrenia may stop taking their medication either because it did not make them better, lack of insight into the illness, belief that it is poison, they had intolerable side effects or they feel they have been stabilized on the antipsychotic drug and feel well enough to discontinue it on their own. Because of the seriousness of schizophrenia, it is best not to stop treatment. If you are a caregiver, family member or friend of the person with schizophrenia, ask him or her to try to take the medication for a specific period of time. Be patient, antipsychotic medication can take weeks or even months to start working at full strength. Once the medication starts to take effect, hopefully, the person will begin to think rationally and start to realize the benefits of long-term treatment. This leads to continuing to take the medication on a regular basis.

Those diagnosed with schizophrenia benefit mostly from taking antipsychotic medication most of their lives. There is no sure way to prevent schizophrenia, but adhering to your treatment plan can prevent relapses or worsening of symptoms. A relapse can occur if medications are discontinued or taken irregularly. Continued drug treatment lessens relapses and reduces the intensity and frequency. Research suggest that the sooner a person with schizophrenia is treated, the better the outcome for the person.

Your doctor will determine which antipsychotic medication is best for you, by taking in consideration the following:

- Cost (how affordable is it).
- What side effects it carries.
- How effective it is in treating your symptoms.
- How readily it can be acquired.
- The dosage and intervals required when taking it.

If the person with schizophrenia has trouble remembering to take his antipsychotic medication, to help ensure that he takes the prescribed medications, he can try a shot which he gets from his doctor once every few weeks or once a month. This is called (LAT) or (LAI) long-acting injectable antipsychotic medications. It is just as effective as taking your daily pill. Some long-acting injectable antipsychotic medications include ones like Haldol, Prolixin and Trilafon.

When taking medications orally, to let you know if you have or have not taken your medication you might use a pill box labeled with the days of the week or a medication calendar. Electronic timers that beep when it's time to take your medication can also be helpful. Having a friend or family member call you to let you know its medication time or taking you medications only at dinner time or bedtime can assure adherence.

SUPPORT GROUPS

The symptoms of schizophrenia can be a very lonely experience. Medication is the foundation. It helps clear up your symptoms and tries to get you back into reality, but it is not the total answer. After the symptoms of schizophrenia are controlled, there are various types of therapy to help one manage their illness and continue to improve their lives. The schizophrenic person might require the support of their families, friends and communities. A strong support system is necessary. Support groups, rehabilitation and family therapy can work wonders in schizophrenia treatments. With such support the person with schizophrenia can learn to cope and live with schizophrenia for the rest of their life.

Family therapy is a useful treatment for schizophrenia, because schizophrenia can affect everyone in the family. Even though your family or friends love you and want to help, having to take care of a person with schizophrenia can be a challenging experience. Because family members or friends may not understand schizophrenia, they along with caregivers should be educated about the disease to be able to help the individual stay with their treatment plan. Family therapy can also decrease relapse rates for the family member with schizophrenia.

The schizophrenia person may have a difficult time performing ordinary life skill as well as communicating with others in the family and at work. Support groups, rehabilitation and psychosocial therapy are beneficial to most people with schizophrenia. A support group can be of help in making the person transition back into daily social life. Many communities have programs to help people with schizophrenia or they can receive help from their local community mental health facility. Psychosocial therapy, rehabilitation and support groups help people learn social skills, help develop life- management skills, find and hold a job, get access to housing, learn money management skills, how to use public transportation, complete educational training, and/or cope with stress or help in Identifying early warning signs of relapse.

Assertive Community Treatment (ACT) provides comprehensive treatment for people with schizophrenia. ACT, unlike other community-based programs, that match the person with mental health or other services, provides highly individualized services directly to the person with schizophrenia. The ACT Team professionals work with and help the person meet the challenges of daily life, address problems, help to prevent crises, and ensure medications are taken properly.

Peer Support Groups help the person with a mental illness like schizophrenia by encouraging their involvement in their recovery by helping them work on social skills with others.

Psychotherapy, a form of talk therapy is also helpful in the treatment of schizophrenia. Research has shown that psychotherapy and medication can be more effective than medication alone, however, psychotherapy alone is not a substitute for medication. Therapy is helpful because it gives one the opportunity to talk about issues that plague them. Individual psychotherapy sessions include a psychologist or therapist and the person with schizophrenia. Sessions meet regularly and focus on the person's thoughts, feelings, relationships or problems. By talking about these issues with a psychologist or therapist the person may gradually come to recognize and understand more about themselves and their problem.

Cognitive Behavioral Therapy (CBT) for schizophrenia is a type of talk therapy between the person with schizophrenia and a therapist. Its aim is to minimize dysfunctional thinking, actions and emotions. It helps develop motivation, to identify the person's goals and strengths. It helps to learn about the illness and learn skills training. CBT helps the person to examine their delusions and hallucinations so as to recognize reality instead of hallucinations and delusions. It helps to eliminate the person's symptoms, and to learn to live with them so that the person can achieve their goals and dreams.

THE TREATMENT TEAM

A treatment team includes a group of skilled mental health professions. The importance of a treatment plan is to ensure that you are getting the proper help you need to aid in your recovery and to help you reach your treatment goals. Your treatment team may include one or all of the professionals listed:

PSYCHIATRIST - A psychiatrist is a medical doctor who diagnoses mental health conditions and prescribe medications.

PSYCHOLOGIST - A psychologist is a trained professional who provides therapy to help someone manage their thoughts better.

OCCUPATIONAL THERAPIST – An occupational therapist helps you set goals base on your interests and abilities to help with your daily life.

PHYSICIAN ASSISTANT – A physician assistant prescribes medications and works under the guidance of a psychiatrist.

NURSE PRACTITIONER – A nurse practitioner diagnoses mental health conditions and can prescribe medication. They are required to work under the guidance of a psychiatrist.

CASE MANAGER – A case manager makes sure that patients receive the care and support they need.

SOCIAL WORKER – A social worker coordinates support and social services for patients.

PHARMACIST – A pharmacist fills your prescriptions, and gives advice on medicines.

There is not a certain way to keep one from having schizophrenia, but adhering to a treatment plan can help by preventing relapses and the worsening of symptoms, improve overall health and make life more fulfilling.

QUESTIONS TO ASK YOUR DOCTOR

If you are experiencing symptoms of schizophrenia and you need to see a doctor, a good psychiatrist or psychologist should be an ally in the process of your treatment and recovery. They are experienced in treating schizophrenia and related disorders. Your doctor should be willing to work with you. Listed are some suggestions in helping you find a psychiatrist or psychologist you can effectively work with:

- Consult with others in the medical profession like your physician.
- Ask friends or relatives who they would see if they had similar problems.
- Contact your local state or county mental health organizations, and ask about good mental healthcare providers.

While any medical professional can make a schizophrenia diagnosis, only a mental health professional, like a psychologist or psychiatrist, is trained in the diagnosis and treatment of schizophrenia.

Once you have selected a psychiatrist and received a diagnosis of schizophrenia, you will probably have many questions. Don't be afraid to speak up. By asking questions and getting the facts you need to know will help you to move forward with your life. Make sure the psychiatrist is aware of all of your symptoms. This will help him to make a correct diagnosis. Some example questions to raise to your doctor are:

1. How many years have you been practicing?
2. Is schizophrenia a disorder that you often treat?
3. What causes schizophrenia?
4. What are the symptoms of this disorder?

5. How is schizophrenia treated?
6. Why have you prescribed (name of medication) for me?
7. Why have you prescribed this dosage for me?
8. Are there any side-effects of this treatment; what are they?
9. How will side effects be managed?
10. After taking the medication, how long will it take before I notice a change in my symptoms?
11. I take other medications. Can I also take the prescribed medication?
12. How often do you review my medication?
13. Can I become addictive to this medication?
14. Is schizophrenia curable?
15. If I don't like this medication. Can I stop taking it?
16. What happens if my treatment is not effective?
17. Will I have to take medication for the rest of my life?
18. How long will I need the treatment?
19. Can I drink alcohol, use drugs or smoke while taking this medication?
20. What effects would medication have on my physical health – how often will this be looked at?
21. Are there other services that could help me?
22. What are the best times and most dependable way to reach you?
23. Where can I reach you if I have an emergency?
24. Can I work or drive with this illness?
25. Do you have a business card and information pamphlet I can have?

Most people with schizophrenia will likely have to be hospitalized at some point during their illness. Rather than outpatient care, a person may need to be hospitalized because they need to be in a protected environment to keep from harming themselves or others; their symptoms and reactions to medication need to be monitored and hospitalization is a safe place for them to stabilize and concentrate on recovery. Being hospitalized gives you more time with your doctor/therapist, most likely every day. Other staff members are around to talk about your concerns or thoughts, and depending on the hospital, there will be group therapy, recreation and vocational/social rehabilitation programs.

The person with schizophrenia can request hospitalization themselves. This is called voluntary admission. Or he can be admitted involuntarily by the decision of the treating psychiatrist, by court order or by emergency staff.

However, admitted, the hospital can be the best thing for your health and well-being.

PART VII

HEALTHY LIVING

THE IMPORTANCE OF HEALTHY EATING

Antipsychotic medication and psychotherapy are normally used to treat schizophrenia. However, eating a healthy diet is also important. Nutrition is very important for people with schizophrenia. As Hippocrates stated, (which couldn't be more accurate in the field of mental health), "Let food be thy medicine, and medicine be thy food."

A psychiatric person cannot be cured, but there are things needed to get the person with schizophrenia well. They are:

- Shelter - (many schizophrenic people are homeless and and cannot get the treatment they need.)
- The schizophrenic person has to be treated with stability, respect and as humans.
- The schizophrenic person must have the right kinds of medication.
- The schizophrenic person must have healthy foods. They must have the right combination of nutrition, vitamins and minerals.

Eating a diet that includes all food groups, eating on a regular schedule, and eating foods in healthy portions are important to help lessen the negative and positive symptoms of schizophrenia.

Research has shown a healthy diet for a person with schizophrenia should include, vitamin B3, antioxidants and omega fatty acids.

Listed below are some tips to help the person eat healthier:

Omega 3 fatty acids (fish oil) has shown some promise for treating and managing schizophrenia. Researchers believe It aids in the functioning of the brain because of its ability to help replenish neurons and connections in affected areas of the brain. In addition to taking medication, people with schizophrenia who take omega- 3 fatty acid or fish oil supplement tend to have fewer symptoms of schizophrenia. Omega-3 fatty acids also support cardiovascular health, support joint health and help to control cholesterol levels.

Foods high in omega-3 fatty acids are essential for brain tissue development and maintenance. Thanks to the omega-3 fatty acids EPA and DHA, have been linked to lower risk of dementia, and improved focus and memory. Fatty oily fish include:

- Mackerel
- Herring
- Salmon
- Tuna
- Trout
- Sardines

Try eating two servings of fish per week. If this cannot be done consider taking fish oil in the form of capsules.

People with schizophrenia have a lessor amount of fatty acids in their brains, so by eating these foods or by taking a supplement can help treat the illness.

- Flaxseeds
- Soybeans

Walnuts - (are the only good nut source of alpha-linoleic acid (ALA) helps promote blood flow, which in turn allows for efficient delivery of oxygen to the brain).

- Olive oil - (a great source of monounsaturated fats, which have been shown to actually slow brain aging).
- Pumpkin Seeds – (also rich in omega-3's, helps to maintain sensory function in the brain).

By consuming foods rich in vitamins and antioxidants in your daily diet, help to fight the free radical causing brain damage. People with schizophrenia go through increased oxidation in the brain. To reduce the amount of oxidation likely to occur in your brain, avoid eating burnt and fried foods. Eating foods rich in vitamins A, C and E can help treat this matter. Antioxidant and vitamin A, C, and E foods may include:

- Oranges
- Avocado (helps facilitate blood flow to the brain because of their high "good" fat and cholesterol contents which Is essential for alertness and focus).
- Watermelon
- Apples
- Mangoes
- Carrots
- Tomatoes
- Peaches
- Berries (mental decline, specifically in memory and focus, is minimized with a diet high in berries).
- Beans
- Plums
- Pecans
- Spinach (rich in the antioxidant lutein; thought to help protect against cognitive decline).
- Wheat grass

Also, to help protect brain cells, eat foods that are rich in vitamin E. Some vitamin E foods are:

- Wheat germ
- Almonds
- Apricots
- Mustard greens
- Peanuts

B vitamins help to lessen the symptoms of schizophrenia and are critical for normal brain function. Folate, B6 and B12 foods act as antioxidants. Adequate levels of Vitamin B3, or niacin improve memory, mood and energy levels and prevents anemia. B vitamins and folic acid are also responsible for maintaining the chemical balance in your brain when taken in an adequate amount. Foods containing the B vitamins are:

- Meats
- Eggs
- Potatoes
- Broccoli

You may consider taking a multivitamin or supplement which can provide sufficient levels of all of the B vitamins. A deficiency in niacin can bring about thought disorders, hallucinations and depression. However, a large dose of niacin daily can help reduce these symptoms. Also, a zinc deficiency can result in many mental illnesses such as schizophrenia. You may take these nutrients in a multivitamin or supplement. Before taking these supplements, consult your doctor to advise you on how much you should take daily.

Mental illness can produce sensitivity to gluten, which can bring on schizophrenic symptoms. To help reduce these issues, try to eliminate gluten sources from your diet. Avoid eating foods like:

- Rye
- Wheat

- Barley (and their by- products)

Because it is difficult to eliminate gluten from the diet, read labels to be sure foods are gluten-free. Gluten sensitivity has improved. Many grocery stores now carry gluten-free pastas, flours, breads and cereals. Common foods to avoid are:

- Bread
- Crackers
- Baked goods
- Beer (and some other alcoholic drinks)
- Soy sauce
- Many cereals

It is best to reduce sugary and carbohydrates intake. Research indicates high levels of dietary sugar increases the risk of both depression and schizophrenia, and worsen symptoms in patients who are already living with schizophrenia and depression. It can make you nervous and jittery. By reducing the sugar intake in diets, people with schizophrenia and depression have shown improvement in energy, mood and clarity. Reducing sugar intake can also promote weight loss, reducing the risk of developing diabetes. Foods to avoid in helping alleviate many symptoms associated with schizophrenia are:

- Candy
- Soda/Pop
- Bread
- Crackers

Limit your caffeine intake. Too much caffeine can make you jumpy and lose concentration.

Dark chocolate is antioxidant-rich and healthy for your whole body. Its caffeine content is thought to play a role in maintaining mental sharpness and focus.

High quality dark and milk chocolate with a high percentage of cocoa solids in it are known to provide memory boosting antioxidants while the milk content can improve motor function and reaction time.

Choose whole grains such as brown rice, if you must eat carbohydrates. Brown rice out shines white rice in all categories. It is nutritional and provides the body with a wide array of vitamins, minerals and antioxidants. It is beneficial for the brain (nerve).

Drink milk in moderation and try to avoid some milk products…. these can aggravate the system. Some people cannot tolerate milk like others.

Limit drinking energy drinks. They can also carry dangerous or unknown side effects that can break your concentration.

Smoothies, a good source of vitamins, nutrients, fiber, water, can be an awesome way to start your day. Add your favorite "brain" fruits, veggies, yogurt, or juice, blend and enjoy the cognitive benefits.

Drink plenty of water. Dehydration can break your concentration.

Try to eat meals at a regular time each day and try not to skip meals. If you tend to forget meals, set an alarm or phone calendar reminder to eat a healthy meal or snack.

Don't forget, each bite of food you consume adds up, so chose healthy foods more often than less healthy foods.

Before starting a nutritional program, consult your psychiatrist, primary physician and/or dietitian.

THE BENEFITS OF EXERCISE

Eating healthy is really, very important, however, physical activity is just as important for people with schizophrenia. Exercise is a main factor in overall health. It is good for the body.

A person with schizophrenia has a shorter life span than people without schizophrenia. It is said that a person with schizophrenia has a life expectancy 25 years shorter than those of the same age, race and socioeconomic background. This is mainly because people with schizophrenia tend to live a more sedentary style of life than the general population.

People with schizophrenia are three times as likely to be obese than those without schizophrenia. A sedentary life style, along with an improper diet and lack of exercise can also cause health concerns such as diabetes, heart disease or hypertension which can be prevented. These illnesses are not caused by schizophrenia. They can develop from the life style one lives.

Medications can also cause a concern. Possible side effects from medications may be weight gain, fatigue, high cholesterol which can also be controlled. Diet and exercise are very important for people with schizophrenia to help control these conditions. Research indicates people with schizophrenia can improve their physical and mental well-being with regular exercise. Exercise can also help to, maintain healthy weight, sleep better at night, and relieve mild to moderate depression symptoms, improve memory, and relieve tension and stress. Exercise increases concentrations of norepinephrine, a chemical that can moderate the brain's response to stress.

You don't have to be a fitness fanatic to reap the benefits of exercising. A moderate amount of exercise can offset some of the risks of being sedentary. Spend less time sitting. Take a walk or head to the gym for a quick workout. When depression and anxiety has robbed you of your energy and motivation to work out or you can't bear the thought of being seen at an exercise class or running through the park. Start small. Schedule your workout time when your energy level is highest. Try dancing to some music or even going for a walk. Any amount of movement is better than none. My doctor tells me that "the human body was designed to move." Try walking laps at a mall, cycling to the store or playing frisbee with a dog or friend. A 15-minute workout will help clear your mind, improve your mood, and boost your energy level. Moving allows you to feel a little better and experience a greater sense of control over your well-being. Whenever you feel energized enough to exercise more vigorously and longer, advance to activities at home, such as gardening or tackling a home improvement project, mow the lawn with a push mower, or sweep the sidewalk or patio with a broom.

Aerobic exercise can help ease schizophrenic symptoms. Research believes that aerobic exercise affects the cognitive functions of people with schizophrenia. Aerobic exercise can ward off cognitive decline, while improving mood and lowering your risk for anxiety and depression. Twelve weeks of aerobic exercise, with 45 to 60 minutes per session has significantly improved the attention and working memory along with greater ability to understand social situations. In combination with medication, aerobic exercise improved overall brain functioning more than people who were treated only with medications.

No matter what type of exercise you take on, exercise rarely happens without a desire to stick with it. Most people perform better when paired up with a workout buddy. This is due to inspiration or good old-fashioned competition. Nobody wants to let the other person down. Find a workout buddy and get moving. Even fitness beginners can inspire each other to push harder during a workout session.

This information is not meant to replace the recommendations of your doctor. Consult with your primary physician or treatment professional before beginning to exercise to be sure you are in good enough health to incorporate an exercise routine into your day.

MEDITATION AND MINDFULNESS

Meditation and mindfulness are often used interchangeably, most often referring to the practice of calming the mind and finding inner stillness. Mindfulness and meditation embody many similarities and can overlap. Many people are turning to meditation today because it is proven to ease anxiety, reduce stress, clear the mind of negative thoughts, fear and worries, making one feel more content. Meditation is especially beneficial for people struggling with schizophrenia. The meditation technique is simply defined as putting yourself in a pause mode through the day and setting aside a time to do a particular meditation. If meditating is done on a regular basis it has been shown to lower blood pressure, and improve sleep quality.

There are many types of meditation. Some examples are:

- Breath-awareness meditation.
- Loving-kindness meditation.
- Mantra-based meditation.
- Visualization mediation.
- Guided meditation.

I have practiced mantra-based meditation/transcendental meditation for years, and it has helped me. This age-old practice is known to have Hindu roots founded by the Indian guru Maharishi Mahesh Yogi (c. 1911-2008). This technique helps me relax in a positive sustainable way, reduces stress, anxiety and helps to lower my blood pressure.

Mantra-based meditation or transcendental meditation is done by using a mantra. A mantra is a syllable, word, or phrase which is repeated during meditation. It can be chanted, whispered, or repeated in the mind. Mantra meditation is a form of mindfulness practice where repetition of the word, phrase or syllable helps settle the mind and allows you to live a more mindful life.

Try taking the time to meditate. It doesn't have to last for hours. Meditation can take 5 minutes, 10 minutes or even an hour. The common misconception on how to meditate is that you must be cross-legged in a yoga pose with your arms bent up and thumb and ring finger touching. Sitting in a lotus position is not necessary today. This can be very uncomfortable. All that's needed is to be in a comfortable position, that allows you to relax and breathe. Meditation can take place sitting on a cushion on the floor, sitting in a chair or even lying down. The main goal is to come to a place where you're settling in and taking the time for you. As with working out, taking time for this self-care practice can do your body and mind a world of good.

One simple seated mantra meditation exercise is to -

- Close your eyes and take one full minute to settle in by taking a few deep cleansing breaths.

- Start to repeat the mantra (word, phrase or syllable you selected) to yourself silently. Slowly synching the rhythm of your breath to the mantra.
- As you inhale, silently repeat your mantra.
- As you exhale, silently repeat the mantra.

Continue breathing slowly and aligning your mantra to your breath, being careful not to rush your breath if you notice your mantra speeding up.

- Each time you notice your mind wander, simply draw your attention back to the mantra.
- When your time is up, gently releasing the mantra, take a moment to sit quietly before opening your eyes.

Mindfulness Meditation is described as a simple form of meditation. It is a type of meditation which involves paying attention to the present moment. When you are mindful, you observe your thoughts and feelings without judging them as good or bad. Mindfulness can be practiced, anytime, anywhere, and with anyone by showing up and being engaged in the here and now. Mindful meditation is advocated for reducing reactions to stress by inducing the relaxation response, lowering the heart rate, reducing anxiety and encouraging positive thought patterns and attitudes. If you have trouble staying focused, try mindfulness meditation. It is a form of meditation or induced relation that focuses awareness on breathing and encourages positive attitudes to achieve a healthy, balanced mental state.

Mindfulness meditation can be as little as a 30 second thing or more than 1 minute.

A simple task like brushing your teeth, or washing your dishes can bring about mindfulness. Tune into your five senses – sight, hearing, touch, smell and taste.

Some Mindfulness Exercises are:

<u>Three hugs, three big breath</u>. Hug someone tight and take 3 big breaths together. Even if they don't breathe with you, your breathing will ground them.

<u>Mindfully eat a raisin</u>. Take a raisin or a piece of chocolate and mindfully eat it. Slow down, sense it, savor it and smile between bites. Purposefully slow down. Use all your senses to see it, touch it, smell it and sense it.

Then gently pop it into your mouth and really savor it. Savor its texture, its taste, how it feels in your mouth. Let it linger and then swallow it. After you have swallowed it, let your lips turn up slightly and smile. Do the same thing for each raisin you eat or bite you take.

<u>Brushing your teeth</u>. You may notice, the flavor of the paste on your tongue.

The smell of the paste coming through your nostrils.
The cooling sensation.
The way the toothbrush moves over your teeth and gums.
The sounds of the bristles moving back and forth in your mouth.
Your reflection in the bathroom mirror and the lighting in the bathroom.
The tingling sensation of the paste on your gums and teeth.

These exercises are meant to help you tune into your surroundings and increase your present-moment awareness which in turn, supports and enriches your ability to be mindful in your everyday life.

Both meditation and mindfulness practices are abilities that help us come to terms with peace internally and externally.

Before starting any meditation technique please check with your doctor and see if it is suited for you. Once you know that it is safe, you may wish to get advice from a professional trainer. Then start meditating.

Mindfulness and meditation can make a big difference in those with Schizophrenia.

PART VIII

SCHIZOPHRENIA AND SUBSTANCE ABUSE

More than fifty-percent of people who suffer with schizophrenia have experience substance use or substance abuse at some point in their lives. Substance abuse is more common among men than women. It is also more common among those in institutional settings like hospitals, jails and homeless shelters.

The use of substances can lead to negative outcomes, such as violence, suicide, homeliness and incarceration. It is shown that people with schizophrenia with substance abuse are also less likely to stick to a treatment plan. Therefore, people with schizophrenia should seriously address the risk of substance use.

Substance use can copy the effects of schizophrenia. Certain substances will make you hallucinate, while others will make you paranoid as well as have disorganized thoughts, similar to symptoms of schizophrenia. With the right support and treatment for substance disorders people can learn to manage symptoms without the use of nicotine, alcohol or drugs. If you or a loved one have a problem with substance abuse, take steps to educate yourself about treatment programs in your community. There are treatments for people who are having trouble with substances, who want to stop using them. If substance use is an issue for you, there is help.

SMOKING

Smoking is the most common form of substance abuse in people with schizophrenia. People with schizophrenia are addicted to nicotine at three times the rate of the average person. 75%-90% of people with schizophrenia are addicted to nicotine compared with 25%-30% of the general population. In the United States, 44% of cigarettes are bought by people with a psychiatric disorder.

Nicotine is the addictive chemical in tobacco. Studies show, people with schizophrenia commonly smoke high-tar cigarettes; and the niche brands are smoked by heavy smokers. Psychiatric facilities report that those patients who are depressed, and those with anxiety disorders smoke in great numbers.

The relationship between smoking and schizophrenia is complex. There has been a lot of research as to why there is a relationship between schizophrenia and smoking.

There are several theories to explain this connection:

Self- medication – Smoking seem to help cope with some of the cognitive symptoms of schizophrenia; it helps them to think clearer and decreases some of the confusions that can happen in schizophrenia.

1. People with schizophrenia smoke to reduce stress, and to reduce symptoms such as depression and agitation.
2. Force of Habit – Smoking nicotine is addictive. People plagued by schizophrenia symptoms are more susceptible to the addictive nature of smoking.
3. Boredom – Many people with schizophrenia often end up being institutionalized for periods of time, or being out of work, or

living an inactive life style. This can lead to a lot of idle time that leads to smoking behavior.

Obviously, we know that smoking leads to a poor outcome. While physicians may not fully understand why people with schizophrenia smoke, we all know that cigarettes kill people.

- Respiratory illnesses, such as lung disease, are one of the leading causes of premature death for people with schizophrenia.
- People with schizophrenia are at higher risk for diabetes. Smoking affects insulin resistance in people with diabetes.
- Smoking causes an increased risk for cardiovascular disease which also causes death in people with schizophrenia.
- Smoking cigarettes can also counteract the effects of antipsychotic medication.

There is substantial evidence that nicotine use through smoking is one of the most dangerous drug problems in the world. Smoking can have a profound social impact on people with schizophrenia. Finance is a major impact. Study reveals that a person with schizophrenia on public aid out of a monthly income of $592 spends an amount of $142 per month on cigarettes. This can result in more social impacts. The person may lack money to spend on entertainment and social events or may not be able to afford housing or nutrition, all of which promote well-being.

Trying to quit smoking can be very difficult for someone with schizophrenia because nicotine withdrawal can temporarily cause a worsening of psychotic symptoms. Nicotine replacement withdrawal strategies may be used to help the person with schizophrenia quit abusing nicotine. Counseling and medications can be helpful. Medications helps people get through the tough phase of quitting. Nicotine replacement therapy (NRT) products that help include patches, lozenges, or using nicotine gum. When the person first quit, there may be withdrawal symptoms because the body is getting used to a life without nicotine. These symptoms are unpleasant but temporary and may include dizziness, anxiety, irritability, trouble sleeping and headaches. An antidepressant drug, bupropion, can be given to relieve the symptoms of nicotine withdrawal.

Giving up smoking is hard to do. But it is possible. When you plan to quit, speak with your doctor or psychiatrist about the best approach for you. Your local city government may be able to provide things like nicotine patches and gum for free.

ALCOHOL

Alcohol is the second most popular substance used for people with schizophrenia. Alcohol is most commonly abused, aside from nicotine. Studies show that up to 30% of people with schizophrenia suffer from an alcohol addiction with more than one-in-three people with schizophrenia being an alcoholic at some time in their life. Alcohol is remarkably easy to procure. In some states it is available in grocery stores. Because it can be gotten so easily, makes it an appealing substance for people with schizophrenia.

Alcohol is strictly forbidden whenever a treatment for schizophrenia has been prescribed. Alcohol should never be consumed because it can conflict with the positive effects of prescription drugs for schizophrenia. The antipsychotics medications may also lose their effectiveness and become neutralized and inert. Therefore, alcohol is strictly forbidden.

Alcoholism is more prevalent in people with schizophrenia than anyone else, because schizophrenic people have additional biological, psychological and environmental factors weighing on them.

"Additional factors that may affect schizophrenia and alcohol abuse include:"

- "Self- medication of the symptoms of schizophrenia and related life factors with alcohol."
- "Encouragement of alcohol use and abuse due to abnormalities in the schizophrenic brain."

- "Easier development of the behaviors that lead to substance abuse due to cognitive impairment typical."
- "Use of alcohol too create a social circle."

Unfortunately, people who have schizophrenia and alcohol abuse issues have poorer treatment outcome, which include:

- More symptom recurrence and more schizophrenia symptom.
- Additional substance use disorders.
- Violence issues.
- Legality problems.
- Medical problems.
- Longevity of time spent in jails and hospitals.
- Suicide attempts.
- Self-harm.

Therapy can help people with schizophrenia to understand that alcohol doesn't help in controlling the disease Therapy may help the person learn how to stop drinking and start working, so they will have better long-term control. Support group work can be helpful. It might help people to connect with others who have this problem and learn how others have control over this very serious disorder.

Alcoholics Anonymous (AA) is an international fellowship of men and women who have a drinking problem. The purpose of the organization is to enable members to stay sober and help other alcoholics achieve sobriety. AA is nonprofessional, self-supporting, and apolitical. The only requirement for membership in the group is a desire to stop drinking. Even the most severe drinking problem can be overcome with the life changing support of Alcoholics Anonymous. Meetings offer real strategies for alcohol rehabilitation and long-term sobriety. AA may be just what you need to overcome your drinking problem. Consult with your treatment team member to advise you on the program.

DRUGS

Drug abuse can be a co-occurring issue among people diagnosed with schizophrenia. Nearly half of all those diagnosed with schizophrenia in the United States abuse drugs or alcohol. Over alcohol, drugs are the most abused substance used by young people.

Marijuana usage has become more accepted in the United States. Several states have legalized the drug for recreational or medical purposes, making it easier to acquire. Analysis of several studies found that marijuana, also called cannabis, is one of the most commonly abused substances among schizophrenics.

Many of the symptoms of Schizophrenia are psychotic, meaning that the person has lost touch with reality. These symptoms include delusions, (persistent false beliefs), hallucinations, (seeing or hearing things that aren't really there). Symptoms may be disorganized thoughts and speech, unusual behaviors, lack of emotion and affect, and reduced ability to function in normal activities. Antipsychotic medications, therapy, and/or social and vocational skills training are used to treat schizophrenia symptoms. However, people with schizophrenia often use marijuana as a way to self-medicate to alleviate the symptoms of schizophrenia, and/or feelings of anxiety and depression.

The relationship between schizophrenia and marijuana is Complex. Marijuana may help some aspects of the condition and worsen the condition in other ways.

For example, some believe that marijuana use can bring about better cognitive performance. This has yet to be proven. Studies have found that a person with schizophrenia can have psychotic symptoms when high on marijuana. Other stimulants such as amphetamines or cocaine use can also exacerbate schizophrenic symptoms and worsen their severity. People with cocaine use disorder are at an increased risk of suicide. These people are more likely to come from low income communities and have had trauma earlier in life.

If you already have schizophrenia and use marijuana, your symptoms may get worse. Based on research chances are higher you will have schizophrenia if you carry certain types of specific genes that affect brain chemistry. The age at which you started using marijuana may also make a difference. Marijuana may also cause schizophrenia symptoms from early usage in life. In your teen years your brain is still developing, therefore your chance of having schizophrenia is greater. If you have a parent or sibling with schizophrenia, your chances are higher in getting the disease.

The exact nature of the marijuana-schizophrenia link is still unclear. Some guidelines to follow before using marijuana are:

- Teens should avoid marijuana or delay using it until they are adults.
- Don't use marijuana if you have schizophrenia.
- Avoid marijuana, if schizophrenia or other psychotic illness runs in your family.
- Encourage the person with schizophrenia to quit using marijuana if you are the caregiver.

Schizophrenia is often mistaken for substance abuse because of the similarity of symptoms. Schizophrenia and substance abuse frequently occur together. Therefore, both disorders are treated simultaneously. If a person stops substance use without being given the proper medication and treatment for mental health, they are likely to relapse. By the same token, if a person is given mental health treatment without taking into consideration substance abuse, they are unlikely to adhere to treatment.

The first step to dual diagnosis treatment is to ensure the person is treated for withdrawal symptoms. This is known as the detox period. Detox enables the medical professionals to determine if psychotic symptoms are being caused by drug abuse rather than schizophrenia itself. After the initial detox and evaluation, dual diagnosis programs are pursued. These programs may involve:

- Cognitive Behavioral Therapy.
- Adult daily living skills training.
- Motivational interviewing techniques.

- Substance refusal skills training.
- Family involvement.
- Medication management.

By treating both disorders together it is believed that this will help the patient improve self-care habits, like sleep and nutrition; and treat other medical conditions which the patient may have developed in conjunction with poor mental health and substance abuse.

PART IX

PRAYER HELPS

Although, prayer can never be a substitute for medication, it is one of the most powerful forces in the world. People often pray because they believe in the power of prayer. It is a way of communicating to God. Prayer is a way of recognizing God's presence is within us, even though we cannot hear him speak to us. Most people pray to ask God for something

A great number of people can attest that prayer has changed lives, saved lives, moved mountains, upheld faith, gotten one through tough times, enhanced your happiness level, can protect you, draw you closer to God and much more.

"Prayer" may be one of those words a person with schizophrenia disorder may not want to hear. However, it's like exercise......physical training is of some value. Prayer may also be of help.

While I am not suggesting that prayer will work for everyone, it helped me with my schizophrenia disorder, along with following my treatment plan.

Prayer will not rid you of hearing voices, but you can find comfort at the most trying time; and peace, a feeling that you are not fighting this battle alone.

It helps to set aside a specific time each day to pray. I find the early hours of the day are best for me to pray. I believe in seeing the face of God every morning before I see the face of man. Don't feel guilty if you miss your intended time or even an entire day for prayer. God has been and will always be in the business for healing. You are not alone. Remember that God always listen. The Lord is always there when you are in need.

Following are some prayers for healing and comfort:

Lord Make New My Mind, Body and Soul

Lord today, I come before you in need of your healing hand,
With you, all things are possible. Renew my mind, body and soul.
I am lost, but I come to you with grace.
From you we have life, and you also give us the gift of infinite joy.
I ask of you strength to move forward on the path you've laid out for me.
Lead me toward better health, and give me the wisdom to identify those
You have placed around me to help me get better.

In Jesus name I pray. Amen.

God watches Over Me

The light of God surrounds me,
The love of God enfolds me
The power of God protects me
The presence of God watches over me
Wherever I am, God is,
And where God is, all is well

Amen

Hope for a Healing

Most gracious and loving Father, thank you for all the blessings you have given me. Thank you, Lord, for waking me this morning and allowing me to see another day of your beautiful creations. You know the state of crisis which I am faced with now Lord. In the time of my hospitalization, you Lord continues to be my rock and my anchor.
You stand as my lighthouse giving me hope. I pray almighty Lord that you will heal me soon.

In your name I pray, Amen.

Relief from Distress

Almighty God, Thank you for your love, grace and mercy. I pray that my discomforts will turn to comforts, my tears to smiles, my pains to gains and my illness to wellness.
I trust in you Lord and in you alone to heal me with any form of skepticism towards blessing that you will be employed upon me.
I trust, Lord, that this agony and suffering that is only in my head, will come to end, and positivism will shine upon me as I read, hear, and study the truth in the Bible.

Amen

Prayer Against Illness

Dear Father, Your scripture says that you heal all diseases and whosoever believe in You will not perish but have everlasting life. Strengthen me, Oh Lord, in this time of illness. When you were on Earth You did all things good and healed all kinds of sickness.

You healed those who had diseases. You died and rose for our sins, so that we may have eternal life. Lord, I believe in my heart that you are here with us today and that your most holy power will remove all sicknesses and evils that roam the earth. Let it be done in Your glory, Dear Lord.

In Your Name I pray. Amen.

The Lord's Prayer

Our Father which art in heaven, Hallowed be thy name. Thy kingdom come. Thy will be done in earth, as it is in heaven.
Give us this day our daily bread. And forgive us our debts, as we forgive Our debtors. And lead us not into temptation, but deliver us from evil. For thine is the kingdom, and the power, and the glory, forever.

Amen

Reading Scriptures from the Bible can be comforting. The Bible says, "By His Stripes We Are Healed." Jesus Christ bore all the sicknesses, infirmities and diseases of the world. He was beaten for our healing. Following are Scriptures on healing:

"But he was wounded for our transgressions, he was bruised for our iniquities: the chastisement of our peace was upon him; and with his stripes we are healed." **Isa. 53.5**

"That it might be fulfilled which was spoken by Esaias the prophet, saying, Himself took our infirmities, and bare our sicknesses." **Matt. 8:17**

"He sent his word, and healed them, and delivered them from their destructions." **Ps. 107.20**

"So that from his body were brought unto the sick handkerchiefs or aprons, and the diseases departed from them, and the evil spirits went out of them." **Acts 19:12**

"And the prayer of faith shall save the sick, and the Lord shall raise him up and if he have committed sins, they shall be forgiven him." **James 5:15**

"And they cast out many devils, and anointed with oil many that were sick, and healed them." **Mark 6:13**

"Who his own self bare our sins in his own body on the tree, that we, being dead to sins, should live unto righteousness: by whose stripes ye were healed." **I Peter 2:24**

"Bless the Lord, O my soul: and all that is within me, bless his holy name. Bless the Lord, O my soul, and forget not all his benefits: who forgiveth all thine iniquities; who healeth all thy diseases." **Ps. 103: 1-3**

"But without faith it is impossible to please him: for he that cometh to God must believe that he is, and that he is a rewarder of them that diligently seek him." **Heb. 11:6**

"And he did not many mighty works there because of their unbelief." **Matt. 13:58**

"So then faith cometh by hearing, and hearing by the word of God." **Rom. 10:17**

"He sent his word, and healed them, and delivered them from their destructions." **Ps. 107:20**

"For a small moment have I forsaken thee; but with great mercies will I gather thee. In a little wrath I hid my face from thee for a moment; but with everlasting kindness will I have mercy on thee, saith the Lord thy Redeemer." **Isa. 54: 7,8**

"And Jesus went about all Galilee, teaching in their synagogues, and preaching the gospel of the kingdom, and healing all manner of sickness and all manner of disease among the people." **Matt. 4:23**

*"And when he saw them, he said unto them, Go shew yourselves unto the priests. And it came to pass, that, as they went, they were cleansed. And one of them, when he saw that he was healed, turned back, and with a loud voice glorified God." **Luke 17: 14,15***

"All that were oppressed of the devil; for God was with him." **Acts 10:38**

"But that ye may know that the Son of man hath power on earth to forgive sins, (he saith to the sick of the palsy,) I say unto thee. Arise, and take up thy bed, and go thy way into thine house. **Mark 2:10,11***

"And when ye stand praying, forgive, if ye have ought against any: that your Father also which is in heaven may forgive you your trespasses. But if ye do not forgive, neither will your Father which is in heaven forgive your trespasses. **Mark 11:25,26***

"Afterward Jesus findeth him in the temple, and said unto him, Behold, thou art made whole; sin no more, lest a worse thing come unto thee." **John 5:14**

*"Bless the Lord, O my soul and all that is within me, bless his holy name. Bless the Lord, O my soul, and forget not all his benefits: who forgiveth all thine iniquities; who health all thy diseases." **Ps. 103:1,2,3***

"But he was wounded for our transgressions, he was bruised for our iniquities: the chastisement of our peace was upon him; and with his stripes we are healed." **Isa. 53:5**

"And said, If thou wilt diligently hearken to the voice of the Lord thy God, and wilt do that which is right in his sight, and wilt give ear to his commandments, and keep all his statutes, I will put none of those diseases upon thee, which I have brought upon the Egyptians: for I am the Lord that healeth thee." **Exodus.15:26**

PART X

MANAGING THE ILLNESS

HELPING YOURSELF

Dealing with schizophrenia isn't easy. It can interfere with your functioning, exert control over your thoughts, and lead to a crisis if not treated. Although, there is no cure for schizophrenia, the outlook for people who have the illness has improved tremendously over the last 30 years. There are treatments that work. Many people improve enough to lead independent, satisfying lives. Following are ways to help you manage your illness:

1. Take Your Medication. Remember, medication(s) can take time to work and provide symptom relief. You and your doctor may have to try a few different options to find the medication(s) that manages your symptoms and works best for you. Even if you are feeling better, taking your meds can help prevent relapses.
2. Establish A Routine. If you follow a routine and that routine breaks down, it is obvious to someone that it is possible you may need to see your psychiatrist or medical doctor, make a change in medication or another form of Intervention. Take

your meds at the same time every day. By doing this it becomes a habit. Use a pillbox or calendar labeled with the days of the week; tape a note to your television channel changer; leave your medication(s) where you can see it or have a family member or friend call you to remind you when it's time to take your meds.

Schizophrenia can make you disorganized. It is possible you may also skip tasks like bathing or doing laundry. A calendar, notebook, or daily diary can help keep you on schedule. Make a list of things you do regularly, and how often they are required. Next make daily, weekly and monthly checklists and set priorities. By doing this helps to prevent a relapse of worsening psychosis, and help keep your mood positive.

3. Eat Healthy and Exercise. A balanced diet and exercise can help raise your mood. Because of the side effects of fatigue, high cholesterol, weight gain and high blood sugar caused by various antipsychotic medications, diet and exercise are particularly important to help keep these conditions under control. Consult with your dietitian, psychiatrist or primary care physician before starting an exercise program or making a dietary change to make sure you are in good enough health to do so.

4. Get Proper Sleep. It is important to get enough sleep. When you're on medication, you most likely need more than the standard eight hours of sleep. Many people with schizophrenia have trouble with sleeping. A lack of sleep is an indicator that an episode of psychosis is developing. Try to go to bed at the same time most nights and wake up at the same time each morning. Monitor your sleep to help make sure your medications are working and that your symptoms are not getting worse.

5. Keep Doctor's Visits. Avoid gaps in care. It has been shown that people with a mental illness die twenty-five years earlier than people without a mental illness. If this is the case, it is wise to take care of other health issues you might have as well. Prevent or control other conditions such a s diabetes, obesity

and depression. People who experience gaps in care are more likely to have relapses, end up back in the hospital and have a reduced quality of life.

6. Avoid Substance Abuse. Avoid drugs, smoking and alcohol. Substance abuse can affect the benefits of medication and worsen your symptoms, and affect your health. Seek help, if you have a substance abuse problem.

7. Know Your Warning Signs. If you can recognize the things that cause you to develop symptoms, you can prepare yourself by either avoiding these things or having an exit plan. It is common for people with schizophrenia to become paranoid around certain people or things; have anxiety in busy social situations; worry about people's motives; hear voices from time to time or have trouble concentrating. Knowing what to look for can help you manage your illness, along with the help of medication and extra support.

8. Meditation and mindfulness can ease anxiety, reduce stress, calm the mind and clear the mind of negative thoughts, fear and worries, making one feel more content. I found meditation to be effective. Before starting a meditation technique please consult with your psychiatrist, primary care physician and/or a professional trainer to see if it's suited for you.

Following these suggestions, may take effort at first to incorporate them into your daily routine. However, once they become a habit you will feel better and be able to enjoy life more. It works for me!

HELPING A FAMILY MEMBER OR
OTHERS WITH SCHIZOPHRENIA

Living with schizophrenia can be challenging. Often times a person with schizophrenia will refuse treatment, believing they do not require psychiatric help and that their delusions or hallucinations are real. Consequently, family or friends may need to take an active role in having them evaluated by a professional. A caregiver or a relative in your life can be a valuable source of support for your treatment. But helping someone with schizophrenia can be filled with many challenges. Naturally, you may want to help out in a way that is not going to be perceived as intrusive or judgmental. Listed below are some ways to offer your support:

1. Before you can help someone with the disorder you will do much better if you understand what schizophrenia is –and isn't. Reading up on it online is a good place to start. There are also books available to assist you in understanding the illness.
2. Accept the person as a family member. Caring, supportive family members can play a vital role in helping the person to regain the confidence and skills needed for rehabilitation.
3. Keep in mind the family did not cause the illness, nor did the person experiencing it. Avoid placing blame and guilt. Instead focus on the future and what can be accomplished to develop supportive living conditions that will enhance the possibility of rehabilitation for the person.
4. Watch for triggers. Help the person to understand and avoid situations that trigger his or her symptoms. By doing so may prevent a relapse or disruption in his or her normal activities.
5. Try to stay calm. Hallucinations seem real to the person with schizophrenia. Don't try to explain they are imaginary. Calmly explain you see things differently, to avoid dangerous or inappropriate behavior from the person.
6. Don't go along with delusional thinking. The person needs to be able to depend on a person who is objective and aware

of what is really happening. Do not argue with this type of thinking or try to point out faulty logic.

7. Do be compassionate. The person may be unable to see that he or she has schizophrenia. Rather than trying to convince the person they have the illness, show your support by helping him or her keep safe, get the therapy they need, and take the prescribed medications.

8. If your loved one develops or have a substance use disorder, help him or her in getting the help they need to quit the habit.

9. Seek support for the person from extended circles. This may include self-help groups, therapists and clergy.

10. Assist, reinforce and teach the person with Activities of Daily Living, such as grooming, dressing, and bathing.

11. Create a specific day-to-day schedule for the person, to keep on track with taking meds, bathing, changing clothes, doing laundry, etc.

12. Encourage consistent sleep. When someone is lacking sleep, more than likely symptoms will become more severe.

13. Help the person to stay on his medication(s). Be sure medication(s) are taken on time and as prescribed. Don't agree with stopping medications because the person thinks he is "cured," or because he says "the medication makes me feel sick." Consult with the doctor first before making any change to medications.

14. See that he or she keeps appointments with their therapist, psychiatrist and/or primary physician.

15. Never say to the person "pull yourself together." If he could, he would. Not being able to do this comes with the illness.

16. Don't wait for a crisis, find out about benefits and support systems for the person in advance when things are going well.

17. Know that taking care of the person with schizophrenia can be draining. Keep yourself physically and emotionally strong. Don't neglect your own needs. Continue your own outside interests. Schedule time for yourself. You are there to provide the support the person who has schizophrenia needs. Remember if you cannot help yourself, you cannot help the person who is in need of your help.

LGBTQ COMMUNITY

It is not uncommon for lesbian, gay, bisexual, transgender or queer (LGBTQ) people with mental illness to find themselves confronted with double stigmas. Many are faced with stigma associated with prejudice because of their gender and/or identity, and discrimination because of their illness. Unfortunately, harassment, family rejection, and civil and human rights denial are sadly common for people of the LGBTQ community. This can bring about suicidal feelings and added mental health struggles for the person.

To assist in overcoming these challenges, early intervention, comprehensive treatment, i.e. consulting with an LGBTQ inclusive therapist can lead to better outcomes. Family support is key to helping LGBTQ people live well with a mental health condition. If you are struggling because of your gender or identity refer to pages 99-104 for more Support Services and Resources.

PART XI

FAMOUS PEOPLE AND CELEBRITIES WITH SCHIZOPHRENIA

Anyone can get schizophrenia. Regardless of social standing or financial earnings it can affect anyone. Even famous people and celebrities have had to deal with this severe debilitating mental illness. If you are reading this book and have schizophrenia, this list can help you know that you are not alone, and that plenty of other individuals have lived with it, some of which are famous and that even people with schizophrenia can be a successful, productive member of society. Below is a list of famous people which have been publicly known and documented as having schizophrenia. "Let's not focus on the negative, but focus on the positive contributions made by people with mental illness."

ADELE HUGO

Adele Hugo is the daughter of renowned French writer Victor Hugo. Her life can be derived from her personal diaries and letters. The schizophrenia illness was also found in other members of the Hugo family. Victor Hugo's brother Eugene also had schizophrenia.

ADOLF WOLFLI

Adolf Wolfli a Swiss artist who was one of the first artists to be associated with the Art Brut or outsider art label. During his childhood he was both physically and sexually abused. Later in life he was convicted of attempted child molestation for which he served prison time. After being freed, he was re-arrested for a similar offense and was admitted to Waldau Clinic psychiatric hospital in Bern where he spent the rest of his adult life. He suffered from psychosis, which led to intense hallucinations.

AGNES BERNICE MARTIN

Agnes Martin was a Canadian-born American abstract painter. Her work has been defined as an "essay in discretion on inward-ness and silence." She was awarded a National Medal of Arts from the National Endowment for the Arts in 1998. She was publicly known to have schizophrenia, once opting for electric therapy for treatment.

ALAN ALDA'S MOTHER

Alan Alda from the highly popularized TV series MASH, mother suffered from paranoid schizophrenia.

ALEXANDER "SKIP" SPENCE

Alexander "Skip" Spence, the Canadian born American musician and singer-songwriter, suffered from schizophrenia.

ALOISE CORBAZ

Aloise Corbaz was born in Lausanne, Switzerland in 1886. She worked as a dressmaker until leaving for Germany in 1911. She found work there as a teacher and a governess, in Potsdam, at the court of German Kaiser Wilhelm II. While there she developed an obsessive romantic passion for Kaiser. Corbaz returned to Switzerland the start of World

War I. Her imaginary romance with Kaiser continued, leading to her being diagnosed with schizophrenia and committed to an asylum. She is known for her drawing and writing poetry, Her work was discovered by Dubuffet in 1947.

ANDY GORAM

Andy Goram is recognized as a former professional Scottish football (soccer) goalkeeper. He played for Oldham Athletic and Hibernian. He is noted for starring for the Rangers during the 1990's and was often referred to as "The Goalie. Andy suffered from a mild case of schizophrenia.

ANTOIN ARTAUD

Antoin Artaud, known as a French playwright, poet, actor and director of theatre, was described as having schizotypal personality features and a psychotic break down later in his life. He spent the remaining years of his life in different asylums and psychiatric hospitals, and was documented as having schizophrenia.

ARTHUR BISPO DO ROSARIO

Arthur Bispo do Rosario was a Brazilian outsider artist, diagnosed with schizophrenia. He lived in a psychiatric institution in Rio de Janeiro for 50 years. While there he began to fashion works of art from different types of material found around the institution. These works were intended to mark the passing of God on Earth, as part of a "divine mission", rather than as art for its own sake. His works gained recognition when they were first displayed at the Venice Biennale in 1995.

ASH LIEB

Ash Lieb, a famous artist, comedian and writer, went through a tough life in the streets and was homeless. He eventually rounded up enough money to treat his schizophrenic condition with the proper medication. He thinks of his art as a primary outlet for his mental illness.

AUDREY MUNSON (AUDREY MARIE MUNSON)

Audrey Munson was an American artist's model and film actress, today considered "America's First Supermodel." She was the model for more than twelve statues in New York City and many others elsewhere. Munson was the first American actress to appear fully nude in the 1915 silent film "Inspiration". In 1922 she attempted suicide and was admitted to psychiatric facilities for treatment. She remained in the St. Lawrence State hospital for the Insane in Ogdensburg, where she was treated for depression and schizophrenia, for 65 years, until her death at the age of 104.

AUGUST NATTERER

August Natterer, also known as "Neter", was a German outside artist with schizophrenia. Natterer, given the pseudonym Neter by his psychiatrist to protect him and his family from the immense social stigma associated with mental illness at the time of his birth on August 3, 1868 in Schornreute, Germany. During his lifetime he got married, travelled widely and had a successful career as an electrician, but was suddenly stricken with delusions and anxiety attacks. In1907, he had a pivotal hallucination of the Last Judgement during which "10,000 images flashed by in half an hour. This ordeal led to suicide attempt and committal to the first of what would be several mental asylums occupied during his life. Natterer thereafter maintained he was the illegitimate child of Emperor Napoleon I and "Redeemer of the World." This vision inspired an intense production of drawings, all documenting images and ideas seen in the vision. Natterer died in an asylum near Rottwil in 1933.

BETTIE PAGE

Bettie Page, a pinup model, spent 20 months in a mental hospital in California and released. She was diagnosed by doctors as having a case of short-lived schizophrenia and a nervous breakdown, but was able to bounce back to normal functioning.

BOB MOSLEY

The rocker, Bob Mosley, is known as the bass player and a premier songwriter for the band Moby Grape. He also developed a solo music career. Mosley was able to continue to create music with his condition – schizophrenia.

BUDDY BOLDEN (CHARLES JOSEPH "BUDDY" BOLDEN)

Buddy Bolden was a famous comet player, and a key figure in the development of New Orleans "rag time" and jazz music. He is also recognized as "King Bolden." In 1907 he was admitted to the Louisiana State Insane Asylum where he spent the remainder of his life incapacitated with schizophrenia.

BRIAN WILSON

Brian Wilson has been considered as one of the greatest singers of all time. Wilson was a former member of the well-known famous group – The Beach Boys. Throughout his life he had various mental illnesses – schizophrenia and schizoaffective disorder. He regained control over his mental illness and continues to perform music.

BUD POWELL (EARL RUDOLPH "BUD" POWELL)

Bud Powell was an American jazz pianist. Powell was a leading figure in the development of modern jazz or behop. He was also a composer, and many jazz critics credit his works and his playing as having "greatly extended the range of jazz harmony." Powell was admitted to Creedmoor

State Hospital in 1948 where he spent eleven months. He adjusted to being in the hospital though in psychiatric interviews he expressed feelings of persecution founded in racism. Powell had a record of previous confinements at other hospitals. After the last hospitalization his piano playing was negatively affected by the Largactil he was taking as treatment for schizophrenia.

BUTCH WARREN (EDWARD RUDOLPH "BUTCH" WARREN JR.)

Butch Warren was an American jazz bassist who was active during the 1950s and 60s. The first time Butch Warren played bass was at home on an instrument left by Billy Taylor, who had played bass for Duke Ellington. Warren began playing professionally at age 14 in Washington, D.C. He appeared on his first recording in January 1960. He recorded for Blue Note Records 1961 to fill the vacancy of a staff bassist. During this job he played with well know figures such as, Herbie Hancock, Miles Davis, Hank Mobley and others. Mental illness and heroin addiction created problems for Warren. He admitted himself in D.C. St Elizabeth Hospital where he was diagnosed paranoid schizophrenia.

CAMILLE CLAUDEL

Camille Claudel was a famous French sculptor and artist of the 19th century. She gained recognition for the originality and quality of her work. Having been diagnosed with schizophrenia, she went on to destroy many of her statues. Being delusional, she accused others of leading a conspiracy kill her.

CHARLES MANSON (CHARLES MILLES MADDOX)

Charles Manson was an American criminal and cult leader. He formed what became known as the "Manson Family", a quasi-commune based in California. He plotted to start a race war and in 1971 he was convicted of first-degree murder and conspiracy to commit murder for the deaths of seven people. Manson served his life sentence at California State Prison in Corcoran. He refused to attend his March, 1997 parole hearing and the panel at that hearing noted that Manson had a "history of controlling behavior" and "mental health issues" including schizophrenia and paranoid delusional disorder, and was too great a danger to be released. Manson died in prison at the age of 83 in late 2017.

CLARA BOW

Clara Bow was a Hollywood superstar actress and an iconic figure that rose to stardom in "silent" film during the 1920's, and successfully made the transition to "talkies" after 1927. She was also a leading sex symbol of her time. Near the end of her career, she became delusional because she experienced pains that had no medical foundation. She was diagnosed with schizophrenia. Bow behaved oddly, but rejected the fact that she was schizophrenic and appeared to function normally.

DANIEL JOHNSTON

Daniel Johnston, a singer, songwriter, musician and visual artist has spent extended periods in psychiatric institutions, was diagnosed with schizophrenia and bipolar disorder. He was the subject of a documentary, "The Devil and Daniel Johnston."

DARRELL HAMMOND

Darrell Hammond, a stand-up comedian, actor and impressionist, is widely recognized as a regular cast member on the show, Saturday Night Live from 1995 to 2009. He is known as the longest tenure of any cast member in the show's history. He has done over 100 celebrity's impersonations. In an October 2011 interview with CNN, Hammond revealed that he had been brutally abused by his mother during his childhood. This trauma from abuse led to cutting himself, several hospitalizations due to psychiatric issues, and diagnoses which included bipolar disorder, schizophrenia, and borderline personality disorder. Hammond admits that he used to cut himself while backstage during a show, and was always on medication during his entire career on Saturday Night Live.

DARREN RAINEY

Darren Rainey born January 12, 1962, died June 23, 2012 at the Dale Correctional Institution in Miami-Dade County, Florida. Rainey had defecated in his cell and refused to clean it, and because of that, prison guards punished him.

It is said that Rainey, who was mentally ill, was fatally tortured by prison authorities by scalding him in a shower for two hours. He died from burns to more than ninety percent of his body. His skin "fell off at the touch." Rainey suffered from schizophrenia.

ED GEIN (EDWARD THEODORE GEIN)

Ed Gein was as American murderer and body snatcher. He is known as the Butcher of Plainfield or the Plainfield Ghoul because his crimes were committed around Plainfield, Wisconsin. He exhumed corpses from local graveyards and fashioned trophies and keepsakes from their bones and skin. He killed two women. Gein was found guilty but legally insane, and was admitted to a psychiatric institution. He died at Mendota Mental Health Institute in 1984.

EDUARD ELNSTEIN

Eduard Einstein, the son of renowned physicist Albert Einstein, was diagnosed with schizophrenia by the age of 20. He was institutionalized two years later for the first of several times. He was a great student and very musically talented before his illness. He struggled with mental illness for the remainder of his life and died of a stroke at 55 years old.

EDWARD CHARLES ALLAWAY

Edward Allaway was a custodian at the California State University. Armed with a semi-automatic rifle he killed seven people and injured two others in the library's first floor lobby and at the building's instructional Media Center, located in the basement. Having a history of violence and mental illness. Allaway was diagnosed with paranoid schizophrenia and found insane by a judge after being convicted by a jury. After a stay at Patton State Hospital, in 2016 Allaway was transferred to Napa State Hospital where he currently lives.

ELYN SAKS

Elyn Saks is a Professor of Law, Psychology, Psychiatry, and Behavioral Sciences at the University of Southern California Gould Law School. She is an expert in Mental Health Law and a MacArthur Foundation Fellowship winner. She experienced her first full blow episode of schizophrenia while attending college.

ELFRIEDE LOHSE-WACHTLER

Elfriede Lohse-Wachtler was a German Expressionist artist/painter associated with the Dresden Sezession artist group and known for her paintings of the city's disenfranchised population. She suffered from mental illness and fell into obscurity after she was murdered by the Nazis during World War II.

EMILE NELLIGAN

Emile Nelligan was a Canadian poet, born 1879. He published his first poems in Montreal at the age of 16. In 1899 he began to exhibit odd behavior. He loudly recited poetry to strangers passing by, and he slept in chapels. He experienced hallucinations and attempted suicide. His parents had him committed to a mental hospital, where he was diagnosed with dementia praecox (now referred to as schizophrenia.)

GENE TIERNEY

Gene Tierney was an American film and stage actress. Acclaimed as a great beauty, she became established as a leading lady. She was best known for her portrayal of the title character in the film "Laura" (1944), and was nominated for an academy award- Best Actress, for her role in the movie (1945) "Leave Her to Heaven." Tierney suffered with schizophrenia.

JACK KEROUAC

Jack Kerouac, an American novelist, poet and writer of French Canadian descent suffered with schizophrenia. He is recognized as one of the most prominent figures of the "Beat Generation." He served in the Navy for an extremely short period of time because of his diagnosis of "dementia praecox" – now day called "schizophrenia"." Kerouac died in 1969 from an abdominal hemorrhage caused by a lifetime of heavy drinking.

JAKE LLOYD (JAKE MATTHEW LLOYD

ALSO KNOWN A JAKE BROADBENT)

Jake Lloyd is an American former child actor, who played Anakin Skywalker in the 1999 film Star Wars: Episode I – The Phantom Menace, the first in the Star Wars prequel trilogy. Lloyd diagnosed with schizophrenia, transferred to a Psychiatric Facility.

JEREMY SAXON OXLEY

Jeremy Oxley is an Australian singer, song-writer and guitarist. He fronted the 1980's pop-rock band Sunnyboys. The band broke up in 1984 due to conflict within, and because of Oxley's health issue-schizophrenia. Oxley went on and formed The Chinless Elite and they released many cover records.

JIM GORDON

Jim Gordon was an American recording artist, musician and songwriter. He was considered a popular session drummer in the late 1960's and 1970's; and was the drummer in the rock super-groups such as Derek and the Dominos, Little Richard and Delaney & Bonnie. He is also a Grammy Award winner. Gordon served 16 years to life in prison for the murder of his mother. In 1983, following her murder, he was classified as living with undiagnosed schizophrenia.

JOE MEEK

Joe Meek, a 1960's English record producer, sound engineer and songwriter, pioneered space age and experimental pop music. He is considered one of the most influential sound engineers of all time. He is mostly remembered from his work with the Tornados "Telstar" in 1962. This was the first record recorded by a British group to reach number one on U.S. charts. Meek lived with undiagnosed schizophrenia. His commercial success was essentially temporary. He eventually became depressed and fell into deep financial debt. He exhibited undiagnosed symptoms of schizophrenia, killed his landlady and committed suicide.

JOHN HINCKLEY, JR.

John Hinckley, an American man, on March 30, 1981 attempted to assassinate the U.S. President Ronald Reagan in Washington, D.C. Hinckley was obsessed with actress Jodie Foster, and tried to assassinate the president in order to impress her. He was found not guilty by plead of insanity and has remained under psychiatric care. His legal representative stated that Hinckley had been diagnosed with schizophrenia, narcissistic personality disorder, schizoid personality disorder, and dysthymia.

JOHN NASH

Dr. John Forbes Nash was an American mathematician known for his genius as well as diagnosis of paranoid schizophrenia. Nash's work has provided insight into the factors that govern chance and decision-making inside complex systems found in everyday life. His theories are widely used in Economics. Servicing as a Senior Research Mathematician at Princeton University during the latter part of his life, he shared the 1994 Nobel Memorial Prize in Economics Sciences. His life is well documented in the book and movie, "A Beautiful Mind."

JOHN OGDON

John Ogdon, an English pianist and composer was known for his musical talents. He is recognized as one of the top musical talents in the world. He made his first public appearance in London at the age of 21 with an hour-long performance of Ferruccio Buson on the piano. Prior to schizophrenia, Ogdon's health was good and physical constitution was strong. His wife Brenda noted this in a book she wrote called "Virtuoso." In 1973, an everyday business argument seemed to upset Ogdon more than expected. He experienced a severe breakdown. His illness was diagnosed as schizophrenia.

KATHERINE ROUTIEDGE

Katherine Routiedge, was a British archaeologist and anthropologist, known to have suffered from a mental illness since childhood which later developed into paranoid schizophrenia. In 1914 Routiedge initiated and carried out much of the first true survey of Easter Island. Because of her illness, many are astonished that she was able to gather so much valuable anthropological research. Routledge became preoccupied with spiritualism and experienced delusions. She was eventually placed in mental institutions.

LIONEL ALDRIDGE

Lionel Aldridge was an American professional football player, a defensive end in the National Football League for eleven seasons with the Green Bay Packers and San Diego Chargers. The Super Bowl winning NFL player also had to deal with schizophrenia. He eventually went on to retire from football in the late 1970's. After being found homeless in Milwaukee, he recognized that something needed to be done about his condition.

LOUIS WAIN

Louis Wain was an English artist, well-known worldwide for his drawings which feature anthropomorphized large-eyed cats and kittens. He slowly regressed with major symptoms of schizophrenia. According to some psychiatrists this can be seen in his works. He was an extremely successful artist. His works still remain published in many pieces of literature.

MEERA POPKIN

Meera Popkin, a high achiever and renowned Broadway star, was diagnosed with mild schizophrenia during her performance as Miss Saigon in the award- winning musical "Cats." She ended up getting locked up in a padded room for a period of time, and has learned to cope with the disorder. Presently she is a huge advocate for mental health awareness. She is married and enjoying watching her baby girl grow up.

NATHANIEL AYERS (NATHANIEL ANTHONY AYERS, JR.)

Nathaniel Ayers is an American musician playing double bass. He is the subject of many newspaper columns, a book, and a 2009 film adaptation based on the columns. In 2008, a foundation was developed in his name aimed to support artistically gifted people with mental illness. He suffered a mental breakdown during his second year at

Julliard School and was institutionalized. After the death of his mother, he moved to Los Angeles thinking his father lived there. Homeless and suffering from symptoms of schizophrenia, he lived and played music on the streets.

PARVEEN BABI

Parveen Babi, was an Indian film actress, model and interior designer. She is most remembered for her appearances in popular commercial films, and for her roles along heroes of the 1970's and early 1980's in movies like "Deewar," "Shaan" and "Namak Halaal." Parveen is regarded as the most beautiful actresses in the history of Hindi cinema. The actress who became a superstar was eventually handcuffed and ankle-cuffed by policemen and removed from an airport for hysteria as a result of her schizophrenia condition. It is believed that she suffered from paranoid schizophrenia.

PETER GREEN

Peter Green is an English blues, rock singer, songwriter and guitarist. He is widely recognized as one of the greatest guitarists of all time. As co-founder of the group Fleetwood Mac, he was inducted into the Rock and Roll Hall of Fame in 1998. Green was diagnosed with schizophrenia in the 1970's and received therapeutic treatments. Attempting to cope with his condition, he spent some time in psychiatric wards and became a recluse for years. Today, he still plays his guitar at live performances.

PHILLIP K. DICK

Phillip Dick was an American writer known for his work in science fiction. His work explored philosophical social and political themes with stories dominated by monopolistic corporations, alternative universes, government dominance, and altered states of consciousness. His work also reflected his interest in metaphysics and theology. It often drew upon his life experiences describing the nature of reality, drug abuse, schizophrenia and transcendental experiences. He is believed to have suffered from schizophrenia, paranoia, and abused drugs in his past.

ROGER KYNARD "ROKY" ERICKSON

"Roky" Erickson, an American musician, singer and songwriter, was the founding member of the 13th Floor Elevators and pioneer of the psychedelic rock genre in 1968. In his performance he began to speak gibberish. Doctors eventually diagnosed him with paranoid schizophrenia. He was placed in a mental health ward where he received electro-shock therapy. Some suspected that LSD, mescaline, DMT, and marijuana may have brought about his condition.

ROSE ISABEL WILLIAMS

Rose Williams is the sister of renowned author Tennessee Williams. It is said that Rose suffered from schizophrenia. This goes to show that even relatives of someone successful can develop this condition. Rose was the model for the character of Laura Wingfield in "The Glass Menagerie" and echoed in many other Williams characters. She died of cardiac arrest at age 86 at a hospital in Tarrytown, New York.

RUFUS MAY

Refus May, a British clinical psychologist who was known for using his own experiences as a psychiatric patient to promote alternative recovery approaches for those experiencing psychotic symptoms. After he had formally qualified as a clinical psychologist, he then disclosed that he had a diagnosis of schizophrenia. He was diagnosed at the age of 18 and was detained in psychiatric care three times. He stated that his psychotic symptoms developed from emotional loss and social isolation. He was hospitalized because of his delusional thinking that he was a spy for the British Secret Service, and having received messages from the radio and television.

REFUS WATSON

Refus Watson is the son of the American molecular biologist, Dr. James Watson.

Dr. Watson is the winner of the Nobel Prize for co-discovery of DNA. He is a strong advocate in understanding and improving the treatment of mental illness. His goal is to determine how genetics has an influence in the development of this condition. His motivation is in part deeply personal. His son, Refus, who is a 38 years old person with schizophrenia lives at home and is unable to cope with the outside world and friends.

SARAH HOLCOMB

Sarah Holcomb, an American former actress, starred in films such as "National Lampoon's Animal House" in 1978, and in "Caddyshack" in 1980. She is noted for her debut role as Clorette Depasto, the daughter of Mayor Carmine DePasto in the movie "National Lampoon's Animal House." Holcomb was only 18 years old at the time of this filming. Unfortunately, her life took a turn for the worse with increased drug abuse, alcohol abuse, and with the eventual onset of schizophrenia.

SYD BARRETT (ROBERT KEITH "SYD" BARRETT)

Robert Keith "Syd" Barrett was an English singer, songwriter and musician, who cofounded the rock band Pink Floyd in 1965. Barrett named the group and was their original lead singer, guitarist and principal songwriter. Characterized for his English accented singing and free form writing style, and his innovative use of guitar techniques, proved influential to many musicians. He was later ousted from the band amid speculation of mental illness and his excessive substance abuse use. There is some dispute as to what kind of mental illness he suffered from but his close friends and band members identified his condition as schizophrenia. He began his solo career in 1968. In 1970, he left the music industry, and lived a relatively quiet life for three decades in a small cottage in England. He is considered as one of the most famous rock stars to ever develop a mental illness.

TED KACZYNSKI (THEODORE JOHN KACZYNSKI)

Ted Kaczynski, also known as the "Unabomber," is an American domestic terrorist, former mathematician professor, and anarchist author. He was a mathematician prodigy. He abandoned an academic career in 1969 to pursue a primitive lifestyle. Between 1978 and 1995 he killed three people and injured 23 others in an attempt to start a revolution against the industrial system. He had views that opposed industrialism and modern technology. Some argue whether he had schizophrenia, but he was formally diagnosed with paranoid schizophrenia.

TOM HARRELL

Tom Harrell, a jazz trumpeter, flugelhornist, composer and arranger, was diagnosed with schizophrenia. He has received many awards and grants throughout his career. He was dubbed as the "greatest trumpeter" of his generation by Entertainment Weekly, and was voted trumpeter of the year in 2018 by the Journalists Association.

VASLAV NIJINSKY

Vaslav Nijinsky, the famous Russian ballet dancer, was recognized as the greatest dancer of the early 20th century. He was known as having great skill due to the detail and intensity of his performances. Many also know him for his incredible leaps. He was a star dancer for the Ballets Russes which showed Russian ballets in Paris. Even with his great success, he developed schizophrenia after going through high amounts of stress. To no avail, he was treated by a psychiatrist in Switzerland. The rest of his life was spent in and out of psychiatric hospitals and various asylums.

VERONICA LAKE (CONSTANCE FRANCES MARIE OCKELMAN)

Veronica Lake, born Constance Frances Marie Ockelman, was an American film, stage and television actor of the 1940's. Lake was best known for her femme fatale roles in noirs film with Alan Ladd in the 1940's and her peek-a-book hairstyle. She experienced a decline in her career as a result of alcoholism and mental illness. According to her mother, Lake had a troubled childhood, and was diagnosed with schizophrenia.

VINCENT VAN GOGH (VINCENT WILLIAM VAN GOGH)

Vincent William Van Gogh was a Dutch post- impressionist painter whose work notable for its beauty, emotion and color highly influenced 20th century art. He is among the most famous and influential figures in the history of Western art. Gogh struggled with mental illness and remained poor and virtually unknown throughout his life. He is thought to have suffered from both schizophrenia and bipolar disorder.

WESLEY WILLIS (WESLEY LAWRENCE WILLIS)

Wesley Lawrence Willis was an American singer-songwriter, and visual artist from Chicago. Willis began his career as an underground singer and songwriter in the outsider music tradition with songs featuring his bizarre, humorous, and obscene lyrics. He started his own punk band called Wesley Willis Fiasco. As a visual artist, long before he developed an interest in music, he is known for creating hundreds of colored ink-pen drawings that depicted the city of Chicago. He was diagnosed with chronic schizophrenia in 1989.

WILL ELLIOTT

Will Elliott is an Australian horror writer known for his novel "The Pilo Family Circus." His debut novel, "The Pilo Family Circus," was published in Australia in 2006 after winning the inaugural ABC Fiction Award (sponsored by ABC Books). Elliott has experienced much literary success, and has since gone on to publish many short stories as well as a book, "Strange Places"- a memoir that documents his experiences with schizophrenia. Elliott dropped out of Law School at the age of 20 when he began experiencing schizophrenic symptoms.

WILLIAM CHESTER MINOR (W. C. MINOR)

William Chester Minor was an American army surgeon and one of the largest contributors of quotations to the Oxford English Dictionary. He suffered from paranoid schizophrenia. He was held in a psychiatric hospital from 1872 to 1910 after he committed a murder and actually cut off his genitalia as a result of being out- of- touch with reality.

ZELDA FITZGERALD

Zelda Fitzgerald was an American socialite, novelist, painter and wife of writer F. Scott Fitzgerald (also a dancer and artist). Zelda was noted for her beauty and high spirits, and was dubbed by her husband as "the first American Flapper." She and Scott became emblems of the Jazz Age, for which they are still celebrated. It is said that Zelda suffered from bipolar disorder and schizophrenia. She was diagnosed with schizophrenia, but most historians believe this was a misdiagnosis and that she actually had bipolar disorder.

PART XII

MOVIES ABOUT SCHIZOPHRENIA

Schizophrenia is a relatively rare mental illness. It results in a person experiencing symptoms, such as auditory hallucinations, delusions, flat affect, and paranoia to name a few. To better understand this illness, many people turn to watching movies.

Many movies on this subject describe the illness in one way or another. For instance, there are multiple symptoms associated with schizophrenia in the movie, A Beautiful Mind. The most common are hallucinations, delusional behavior and trouble focusing. I have listed movies which are about cases of schizophrenia or are thought to be on schizophrenia. A few of these movies were released dating back as far as 1948. Some of the movies are fiction, and some are based on true stories of a person dealing with the illness.

<u>MOVIE LIST</u>

The Snake Pit – 1948
The Caine Mutiny - 1954
Through a Glass Darkly – 1961

Repulsion - 1965

Images – 1972

No Mercy No Future (Die Beruhrte) – 1981

After Darkness – 1985

Promise - 1986

Drop Dead Fred – 1991

The Fisher King – 1991

Me, Myself And I - 1992

Clean Shaven – 1993

Benny & Joon – 1993

Angel Baby – 1995

Conspiracy Theory – 1997

Pi - 1998

Julien Donkey-Boy – 1999

The Messenger: The Story of Joan of Arc – 1999

A Beautiful Mind – 2001

Donnie Darko – 2001

The Caveman's Valentine – 2001

K-PAX – 2001

Revolution #9 - 2001

Igby Goes Down – 2002

Spider – 2002

Homeless to Harvard: The Liz Murray Story – 2003

Keane – 2004

Spider Forest – 2004

Stateside - 2004

15 Park Avenue – 2005

Shabd – 2005

Proof – 2005

Stateside – 2005

A Scanner Darkly – 2006

Bug – 2006

Canvas – 2006

Memoirs of My Nervous Illness – 2006

Danika – 2006

I'm a Cyborg, But That's OK – 2006
Reprise – 2006
Woh Lamhe – 2006
My Name Is Alan and I Paint Pictures – 2007
Savage Grace – 2007
The Soloist – 2009
Black Swan - 2010
Karthik Calling Karthik – 2010
Shutter Island – 2010
Take Shelter – 2011
Sucker Punch – 2011
Of Two Minds – 2012
Maniac - 2012

Hopefully, at least one of the listed movies will help you to understand schizophrenia better and how it can affect one with the disease.

PART XIII

SCHIZOPHRENIA MYTHS AND FACTS

Schizophrenia is not often spoken about. Because of the lack of knowledge and understanding of this illness, there is a great deal of stigma and incorrect information about schizophrenia. There need to be more awareness about this mental illness. Here are ways to correct schizophrenia myths and stigmas.

Below are some myths, followed by the facts, relative to schizophrenia:

Myth 1

Schizophrenia means that a person has several different or multiple "personalities."

Fact

Schizophrenics do not have more than one personality. Instead, he has false ideas or has lost touch with reality. Multiple personality is a separate brain disorder known as Dissociative Identity Disorder (DID), which in itself is a separate condition, and is treated as such. As with any physical or mental illnesses, schizophrenia can lead to the development of other issues, but it is by no means destined to be multiple personality disorder or several different personalities.

Myth 2

People with schizophrenia are violent. They are a threat to themselves as well as to others.

Fact

Individuals with schizophrenia are no more violent than the general population. Even though the individual can act unpredictably at times, most suffering from the illness are much more likely to be victims of violence, not perpetrators, especially if they are being treated for the illness.

Myth 3

People with schizophrenia are not intelligent and are slow learners.

FACT

People with schizophrenia have all levels of intelligence. It's true that some people with schizophrenia have a harder time learning. Some people with schizophrenia do have difficulty with certain mental functions, as with attention completing exams testing, memory, and learning ability. This hardly means that schizophrenics lack intelligence or creativity. John Nash, a Nobel Prize-winning mathematician, whose life was captured in the movie A Beautiful Mind, was diagnosed with schizophrenia. Vaslav Nijinsky, a Russian ballet dancer had schizophrenia…just to name a few.

Myth 4

People with schizophrenia belong in the hospital.

Fact

In the past, people with mental illness like schizophrenia were sent to insane asylums and mental hospitals, where they incurred painful and inhumane treatment. Now that experts know more about schizophrenia, fewer people need to be placed in long-term mental health facilities. Many individuals with schizophrenia do well living in the community with outpatient treatment. Most live with family or in supportive housing, such as a group home, or assisted living homes, in the community. Medications and living with the community help in the treatment process.

Myth 5

Getting and holding a job is impossible for a person with schizophrenia.

Fact

People with schizophrenia who receive the right treatment have little trouble in getting, keeping and doing well in a job. Many can find a position that fits their skills and abilities with the right treatment. Today employers have developed progressive policies on the hiring of people with mental health disorders.

Myth 6

Schizophrenics tend to get lazy.

Fact

Because of the symptoms of schizophrenia, many people find it hard to go about their daily needs and self-care such as bathing and dressing. This could be said about anyone with a serious condition affecting their mental or physical health. This is not laziness. Help with their daily routine is needed.

Myth 7

People with schizophrenia will never recover.

Fact

With the right medicine and therapy, many people can get recovered and others will see improvements in their symptoms. With proper treatment most people with schizophrenia can live life productively.

Myth 8

I will develop schizophrenia because my mother is schizophrenic.

Fact

Even though genetics play a role in the development of schizophrenia, this does not mean that every off-spring of a schizophrenic person is destined to develop it. The risk of having schizophrenia is about 10%. More than one family member with schizophrenia raises your risk.

Myth 9

Most schizophrenics live on the streets or in psychiatric hospitals.

Fact

About two-thirds of Americans who have a mental illness live in the community, either with their family or in a community living settings.

Myth 10

A person can recover from schizophrenia by thinking positively and praying.

Fact

Recovery is possible when the individual receives treatment and supportive services. Prayer comforts.

Myth 11

People with schizophrenia or an addiction must smoke to manage their symptoms.

Fact

People with schizophrenia do not need to smoke to manage their stress, mental illness or addiction.

Myth 12

People with schizophrenia and addictions can never quit smoking.

Fact

People with schizophrenia can quit smoking with cessation treatment.

Myth 13

Nicotine Replacement Therapy (NRT) is harmful and causes disease.

Fact

Nicotine Replacement Therapy is safer than cigarettes.

Myth 14

Only one Nicotine Replacement Therapy (NRT) product can be used at a time.

Fact

NRT products can be used in combination or alone.

Myth 15

Nicotine Replacement Therapy (NRT) is meant only to be used by healthy people.

Fact

Most people can use NRT through the direction of your doctor.

Myth 16

I will experience no cravings or withdrawal symptoms from quitting smoking when I use Nicotine Replacement Therapy (NRT).

Fact

All of the withdrawal symptoms may not be eliminated completely, however NRT does reduce the withdrawal symptoms associated with cigarette smoking.

Myth 17

Cigarette nicotine and Nicotine Replacement Therapy (NRT) products are the same.

Fact

The products are different, and the livelihood of addiction to NRT is very low.

Myth 18

Nicotine Replacement Therapy (NRT) can't help me.

Fact

NRT does work. Chances of quitting smoking is doubled by using NRT.

Myth 19

Primary care physicians are the only ones who can treat a tobacco use disorder.

Fact

Cessation treatment can also be provided by mental health and addiction clinicians.

Myth 20

Nicotine Replacement Therapy (NRT) is too costly.

Fact

NRT is used for a limited time only, whereas cigarettes are consumed many years. Compared to the price of cigarettes, NRT is less expensive.

PART XIV

USEFUL SITES AND RESOURCES FOR LEARNING ABOUT AND LIVING WITH MENTAL ILLNESS – SCHIZOPHRENIA

WEBSITE, SUPPORT & RESOURCES

www.afsp.org

The American Foundation for Suicide Prevention raises awareness, funds scientific research and provides resources and aid to those affected by suicide. If you are in crisis call The National Suicide Prevention Lifeline at 1-800 273-TALK (8255) or contact the Crisis Text Line by texting TALK to 741741.

www.psychiatry.org

The American Psychiatric Association includes an organization of psychiatrists working together to ensure humane care and effective treatment for all persons with mental illness, including substance disorders. For APA Customer Service Assistance call 1-888 35-PSYCH or 1-888 357-7924. Callers outside the U.S. and Canada call 1-202 559-3900.

www.nmha.org or **www.mhanational.org**

1-800 969-6642 - Mental Health America is the nation's leading community-based nonprofit dedicating to addressing the needs of those living with mental illness and promoting the overall mental help of Americans.

www.Caregiver.org

1-800 445-8106 - The Family Caregiver Alliance is a nationwide public voice for caregivers of loved ones with chronic health conditions.

www.healthyminds.org

Healthy Minds is the American Psychiatric Association's online resource for anyone seeking support or facts about mental illnesses.

www.bazelon.org

1-202 467-5730 - The Bazelon Center for Mental Health Law handles general legal issues. 1101 15th St. NW, Suite 1212 – Washington, DC 20005

www.mhselfhelp.org and **www.cdsdirectory.org**

The National Mental Health Consumers' Self-Help Clearinghouse offers referral, support and information services on mental illness.

Email: selfhelpclearinghouse@gmail.com

www.samhsa.gov

The Substance Abuse and Mental Health Services Administration's aim is to reduce the impact of substance abuse and mental illness on America's communities. The National Helpline, 1-800 662 HELP (4354)/TTY: 1-800 487-4889 provides 24-hour free and confidential referrals and information about mental and/or substance use disorders, prevention, treatment and recovery in English and Spanish. For general questions for mental and substance use disorder, call 1-877 SAMHSA-7 (726-4727)/TTY:1-800 487-4889 or Email: samhsa@samhsa.hhs.gov.

www.szmagazine.com

1-800 493-2094 or 1-240 423-9432 - The SZ magazine on mental wellness provides mental health news and science-based reviews. Email: info@sardaa.org.

www.healthyminds.org/more-info-for/hispanicslatinos.aspx

Healthy Minds, the American Psychiatric Association's online resource, provides support and facts on mental illness for Hispanics/Latinos.

www.nami.org

1-800 950-NAMI (6264) – The National Alliance on Mental Illness (NAMI) supports people with mental illness and their families and friends.

www.nami.org/multicultural

1-800 950-NAMI (6264) – The National Alliance on Mental Illness (NAMI) Multicultural Action Center supports people of diverse backgrounds who are affected by mental illness.

www.janssen.com

1-800-JANSSEN - This site offers information about treatment options for mental illness provided by Janssen Pharmaceuticals, Inc.

www.apa.org/pi/lgbt/resources/lgbt-health

1-800 374-2721 or 1-202 336-5500 - The American Psychological Association (APA) provides a variety of educational and support resources on a range of LGBTQ topics.

www.aglp.org

1-215 222-2800 - The Association of Gay and Lesbian Psychiatrists offers resources for LGBTQ individuals experiencing mental health conditions and offers an online referral system in your area. The AGLP National Office is located at 4514 Chester Ave., Philadelphia, PA 19143. Email: info@aglp.org.

www.transequality.org

1-202 642-4542 – The National Center for Transgender Equality which is the nation's leading social justice advocacy winning life-saving change for transgender people, offers resources for transgender individuals, including information on the right to access health care. Located at 1133 19th Street NW, Washington, DC 20036.

www.glbtnationalhelpcenter.org

The LGBTQ National Help Center, servicing the lesbian, gay, bisexual, transgender, queer and questioning community provides free and confidential peer-support and local resources through phone, text and online chat.

LGBTQ National Hotline – 1-888 843-4564

LGBTQ National Senior Hotline – 1-888 234-7243

LGBTQ National Youth Talk Line – 1-800 246-7743

www.glma.org/index.cfm

1-202 600-8037 - The Gay and Lesbian Medical Association (GLMA) is a national organization committed to ensuring health equality for LGBTQ healthcare professionals. Located at 1133 19th Street NW, Suite 302, Washington, DC 20036. Email: info@glma.org.

www.uptodate.com/contents/quitting-smoking-beyond-the-basic

This site provides links on smoking pertaining to the benefits of quitting, preparing to quit, medications for quitting and other forms of tobacco.

www.cdc.gov/tobacco/quit-smoking/cessation/2019

1-800 232-4636 – The Centers for Disease Control and Prevention (CDC) Office on Smoking and Health (OSH) is the lead federal agency for comprehensive tobacco prevention and control. The OSH saves lives and saves money by preventing and reducing tobacco use.

www.smokefree.gov

This site provides tools and tips to help you quit smoking, and articles and information on smoking. It also provides Live Online Chat.

National Council on Alcoholism and Drug Dependence

1-800-622-2255 – The NCADD helps with drug and alcohol dependence.

www.aa-intergroup.org

The Online Intergroup Alcoholics Anonymous services include an online meeting directory to help locate meetings near you. It also offers email, chat, audio, forums and online meetings in a variety of languages.

Americans with Disabilities Act (ADA)

1-800 514-0301/TTY: 1-800 514-0383 – The U.S. Department of Justice provides information about the Americans with Disabilities Act (ADA). Located at the U.S. Department of Justice – Civil Rights Division, Disability Rights Section – 950 Pennsylvania Avenue NW, Washington, DC 20530.

National Suicide Prevention Lifeline – 1-800 273-8255 (1-800 273-TALK).

National Hope Line Network – 1-800 784-2433 (1-800-SUICIDE).

Suicide Prevention Line Aimed at Gay and Questioning Youth – 1-866 488-7386

(1-866 4U -TREVOR).

<u>Michigan Statewide Mental Health Hotline</u>

9-8-8 - The Michigan Mental Health Hotline is a crisis and access line for people in need of immediate mental health services – available 24/7.

<u>www.veteranscrisislline.net</u>

1-800-273-8255 or Text a message to 838255. The Veteran Crisis Line, operated by the Department of Veterans Affairs, aids veterans and their families who may be in crisis by connecting with VA responders.